Dear Sara & Christopher

Merry Christmas 2015

Looking forward to a great
2016 to us all.

Love
Fox xx

SPECIAL · DELIVERY ·

FAVOURITE
FOOD TO
MAKE &
TAKE

ANNABEL CRABB & WENDY SHARPE

MURDOCH BOOKS

For Christobel *AC*
For Michael *WPS*

Contents

Introduction

Food is a language. Within its rolling landscape of dialects and exotic tongues, so many things can be said.

In my accidental second career as the host of a political cooking show, I take dessert to the homes of politicians, and the message of the dessert is clear, or I hope it is: 'I come in peace.' (They cook for me, too, of course, which is the main game. Usually with great enthusiasm, though it's a long filming day, and occasionally towards the end I'm sure I detect a note of: 'Okay, lady. You and your fleet of cameras can leave any time now.')

But the best things ever said by food are conveyed in quiet tones, between friends and family, when the message is so much more than just, 'Here's a casserole.' It's 'I care enough about you to spend a bit of time making something delicious that you can eat immediately, or put in the fridge and have later, or even better that I can also have a bit of while we open the nice bottle of red that I have – what do you know! – also brought in my basket.'

Tanya Plibersek once told me that cooking big dinners for her friends and family was a way of telling them that – even though she wasn't always around – they were important to her, and worth lashings of her time. And time is the issue here, isn't it? If you're a busy person, then spending time making something for someone you care about is more than a gesture. It means 'I know you are worried about your mum' or 'I know you have invited twenty people over for lunch and, while I do not for one second doubt your ability to cope, I thought this fresh bread might help.'

Food isn't necessarily a big language; it doesn't have the hyperbolic peaks and troughs of Italian, or German's guttural heft. Sometimes, it is the most rudimentary *lingua franca*. A jar of muesli. Or a single serving of soup on a workmate's desk. It can be quiet. But it can say a lot.

My oldest friend in the world is Wendy Sharpe. We met when we were toddlers, in the Adelaide Plains town of Two Wells, in South Australia. My memories of her, even from the early days, are food-related. The day she brought a mango to school (a rare and exotic thing for 1970s Two Wells). The day we cooked spanakopita with our Greek teacher. Cooking with our own mothers and aunties for shearers' smokos; epic catering events, nourished by trays and trays of the sorts of cakes and slices you could never not want to eat. Sleepovers at Grandma Bennett's house, making tortellini alfredo and nicking peaches from the bottom fridge. My mum, Christobel, making Wendy's wedding cake – a croquembouche that Mum rehearsed in various weather conditions so thoroughly that for a while you couldn't enter a shed on the farm without finding a few stray choux buns practising being exposed to heat.

Over the years, we've sometimes lived in the same city (Adelaide, London, Sydney). And when this happens, we strive to live within streets of each other, so as to facilitate the tottering transit of cakes, pies and structurally inadvisable salads. When my first baby was born in London, Wendy provided a full week of flawless in-home catering: a neatly packed basket slipped inside the door to our flat, twice daily. The first dish – an oven-ready mushroom and gruyère tart – I can still taste today. Thus was a post-partum catering tradition born between us; six lovely children, and countless deeply appreciated dishes.

For the last five years or so, we've lived in different hemispheres. This is a serious bummer, as we cannot cook for each other any more, or not without attracting strong interest from the Customs service anyway. But food is still a good language. Our email exchanges are relentlessly food-related. Wendy, who by training is a scientist and a technical editor, bombards me with chemical explanations of why things taste good or why they go soggy in the fridge. She is an experimental, natural, perceptive genius in the kitchen, and the nicest things I ever cook tend to come from her ideas. Ditto the nicest desserts on *Kitchen Cabinet*, for which Wendy is an enthusiastic consultant. Sometimes she really has to talk me into something – like the lemon verbena posset – and then, when I finally relent and make it, it's so confoundingly fabulous that I feel like a goose.

This book was written by correspondence. It's a selection of many things Wendy and I have taken to each other's houses, and some we would have taken if we didn't live on different sides of the damn world. Plus dishes that have said 'Congratulations' or 'Cheer up' or 'Lord, this meeting might be grim – let's have some cake while we're at it' to countless of our friends and family and workmates; and some that have said 'Open up and let me in!' to politicians. It was written, in English, about a language far more global in scope. I hope you enjoy it.

Annabel Crabb

There may be some cynics out there, wondering why a political journalist has written a cookbook. And asking, not very quietly, can that Crabb woman actually cook? Well, the answer is – yes, she can! And really, really cook. Of course, she does the basics: a tasty pasta bake, an impeccable soup, and her work with gingerbread is peerless. And, for heaven's sake, she bakes to relax. But what Annabel specialises in is the complicated, bordering-on-impossible dish. She is never happier than when attempting the culinary equivalent of the 4½ reverse pike off the 3-metre diving board. The polenta-dusted, 20-cent-piece-sized English muffins for Lilliputian quail-eggs benedict? That was just the *start* of her teeny-tiny-food phase.

At the other end of the scale, there was Quercyan cake. Any dish that requires moving the sofa in order to create enough floor space to assemble it can only be filed under 'f' for 'folly'. After the making and rolling out of a vast swathe of translucent pastry, she sprinkled it with filling, rolled it tight and then coiled the lot into a huge tin. It took a day. (Coincidentally, a decade on, I moved to a place a few kilometres to the north of Quercy, and I could not find a single soul who had ever heard of such a cake.)

Yes, the gritty culinary ambition is impressive, but perhaps the very best thing about Annabel's cooking, if you happen to be a friend, neighbour or colleague, is that she doesn't so much cook to eat; she cooks to give. While she may lack a sweet tooth herself (sugar would only distract from her trinity of true loves – the salty, the smoked and the citrusy), there'll always be a zip-lock bag of biscuits, or a wrapped slab of cake thrust into your handbag if you happen to drop by after one of her baking 'relaxation' sessions.

And here is the salient message, the thing that I have learnt from Annabel – cooking is not just about servicing one's own love of tasty food (because that's why I got started in the kitchen). The fun part can be the thrill of giving, of helping, of sharing. And of connecting. In the various countries and cities and towns that I have called home, food has always been the link that has joined me up with people when I knew no-one. Everyone needs to eat, right? Then why not cook for them? Don't be nervous about your culinary skills, or perceived lack of them. Because, as my grandmother always used to say, 'food tastes best when someone else cooks it for you'.

I hope you enjoy this collection of recipes that Annabel and I, or our families and friends, have been giving, receiving, sharing, eating, drinking and enjoying for years.

Wendy Sharpe

Drop-off breakfast

Scandinavian cinnamon buns

If you are incapable of walking properly in those supposedly comfortable Swedish wooden-soled sandals, and that Arne Jacobsen chair is out of your budget, do not despair. These aromatic sweet breakfast treats are an accessible, affordable and tasty road to Destination Scandi-chic. That said, they are a somewhat long road; they need to be started the night before.

Makes about 12

1 teaspoon active dried yeast
45 g (1½ oz) caster
  (superfine) sugar
70 ml (2¼ fl oz)
  lukewarm water
200 g (7 oz/1⅓ cups) plain
  (all-purpose) flour
pinch of salt
1½ teaspoons
  ground cardamom
1 egg
40 g (1½ oz) butter, plus extra
  melted butter for glazing
1 egg, lightly beaten
1½ tablespoons ground
  cinnamon, plus a little
  extra for dusting
175 g (6 oz/1 cup) raisins
icing (confectioners') sugar,
  for dusting

TO TRANSPORT
Although best eaten warm, these cinnamon buns are good for a few hours after baking. Carry in a basket (so the warm buns don't steam and become soggy) and cover with a clean tea towel to keep fresh en route.

The day before, mix the yeast, 1 tablespoon of the sugar and the water in a medium bowl and stir until the sugar has dissolved. Stir in half the flour, then leave to stand for about an hour, or until roughly doubled in size. (This first step is not strictly necessary. You can just let the yeast activate with the water and sugar for 5–10 minutes; however, in my experience, you end up with a fluffier bun if you make this pre-dough beforehand.)

Meanwhile, in a large mixing bowl, combine the remaining flour with the salt and cardamom. When the pre-dough is ready, add it to the flour, along with the egg. Mix until you have a dough. Put the butter between two sheets of baking paper and bash it with a rolling pin to soften it. Fold the butter into the dough and knead until fully incorporated, then cover and rest for 10 minutes. Knead the dough again, then cover and rest for another 10 minutes. Repeat once or twice more, until you have a firm, smooth ball of dough. Cover the bowl and refrigerate overnight. (I realise all this may seem time-consuming, but it is easily incorporated into a quiet evening of box sets, podcasts or late-night radio.)

Next day, knock back the dough and turn out onto a lightly floured bench. Flatten the dough into a rectangle about 25 x 10 cm (10 x 4 in). Brush with the beaten egg, then sprinkle over the remaining sugar, followed by the cinnamon and raisins. Roll up the dough into a long sausage, like a Swiss roll, then cut into slices about 2 cm (¾ in) thick – you should get about 12. Nestle the slices into a greased 23 cm (9 in) baking dish or tin, cover with a tea towel and leave until roughly doubled in size, about 1–1½ hours.

Preheat the oven to 200°C (400°F) and sit a heatproof bowl or roasting tin on the lowest shelf. Put the buns in the oven, pour a cup of water into the bowl or tin; quickly close the door afterwards and reduce the temperature to 180°C (350°F). Bake the buns for 10–15 minutes until golden, then turn out onto a wire rack to cool. While still warm, brush with melted butter, then dust with icing sugar and a little more cinnamon.

Drop-off breakfast

Granola

There are few more welcome gifts than a jar of homemade granola, ready for your happy recipient to disgorge and eat with yoghurt, fruit, berries, cup of tea and newspaper. The ingredients below will give you a nice fruity, nutty, seedy blend, but of course you should not hesitate to personalise it further by subbing in other stuff (alternative nuts, seeds, coconut, freeze-dried strawberries or anything else that steams your beans). This recipe gives a not-too-sweet, quite lightly toasted result, so you might want to add more maple syrup or honey if you have a sweet tooth.

Makes 750 g (1 lb 10 oz)

100 ml (3½ fl oz) maple syrup or honey, or a mixture
2 tablespoons neutral-flavoured oil, or butter
400 g (14 oz) rolled (porridge) oats
1 tablespoon soft brown sugar
100 g (3½ oz) nuts, such as almonds, hazelnuts, walnuts
50 g (1¾ oz) sunflower seeds
50 g (1¾ oz) chopped dried apricots
50 g (1¾ oz) sultanas
50 g (1¾ oz) chopped dried cranberries

TO TRANSPORT
Pack the cooked granola into jars and hand it out to the deserving.

Preheat the oven to 150°C (300°F).

In a small saucepan, combine the maple syrup or honey with the oil or butter and heat until everything is very runny. This step is essential if you are using honey; less so with maple syrup, but I still find that using a hot liquid to coat the oats gives a better result.

Put the oats in a large bowl and mix with the sugar. Pour in the hot sweet stuff and oil or butter and stir until the oats are all slightly damp. Now spill the coated oats out onto two large baking trays.

Cook in the oven for 10 minutes, then add the nuts and give everything a good mix around, breaking up any clumps of oats. Return to the oven for another 10 minutes. The mixture should be lightly golden, but it won't be crispy yet – that only happens when it cools.

Remove from the oven, mix in the seeds and dried fruit, then leave the granola to cool completely.

Bircher muesli

Wendy tried for years to sell me on the merits of Bircher muesli, but I proudly resisted. I have never really embraced intentionally soggy food, with the possible exception of Italian bread soup. But she waited me out, and after the birth of my second child she brought me a batch, sweetening the deal with some toasted almonds. In my weakened state, I succumbed.

The original recipe for Bircher muesli, dreamed up by Swiss doctor Maximilian Bircher-Benner, called for a lot of apple, a few soaked oats, condensed milk and a squeeze of lemon. I can only imagine that it must have been like eating the contents of the paper-recycling tub after it had been left out in the rain all night. This version might be a bit on the indulgent side for the spartan Dr Max, but it makes for good breakfast eating.

I think breakfast foods are sorely neglected in the bring-a-plate category. A nice big jar of this Bircher muesli is certainly something I would be very happy to score from a drop-in guest. Just a word of caution: this might not be the best thing to bring on a first dinner date – it might look like you're assuming you'll be there for breakfast, and that could quickly get awkward.

Serves 6

250 g (9 oz) rolled (porridge) oats
500 ml (17 fl oz/2 cups) milk
125 ml (4 fl oz/½ cup) thin (pouring) cream
125 g (4½ oz) plain yoghurt
100 ml (3½ fl oz) fruit juice – whatever you have on hand
70 ml (2¼ fl oz) maple syrup or runny honey
100 g (3½ oz) dried fruit, such as sultanas, cranberries, chopped apricots
50 g (1¾ oz) sunflower seeds
2 apples, cut into matchsticks – or coarsely grated, if you're pushed for time
2 oranges, segmented (see page 34) and chopped
1 tablespoon lemon juice
50 g (1¾ oz) slivered almonds

As the oats are soaked overnight, you need to start this the day before, but if you have a set of electronic scales, it's a doddle: just add each ingredient, tare, add the next, repeat… and before you can say 'Switzerland's best export', you're done!

Put everything except the almonds in a large bowl, mix well and leave in the fridge overnight. Give the almonds 6 minutes in a dry frying pan over low–medium heat until they are just taking on colour, then set aside for the morning.

Serve the muesli the next day, with the almonds sprinkled on top. Feel free to add any fresh fruit you have lying about.

TO TRANSPORT
Drop this off in a large bowl, or a straight-sided preserving jar (so you can get a spoon in there). It will keep in the fridge for 2 days.

Date and walnut bread

This is a 'bread' in the same way that banana bread from smart coffee shops is a 'bread'. Deep down, we all know that what we're talking about here is cake – but if the rebranding makes us feel okay about eating such deliciousness for breakfast, let's go with it. This recipe is from Wendy's grandmother's recipe book, only with a little less sugar and a sub-in of half wholemeal flour. As anyone who lived through the 1970s in Australia will know, it absolutely must be eaten slathered with plenty of cold butter.

Makes 1 large loaf,
or 2 smaller ones

60 g (2¼ oz) butter
160 g (5¾ oz/1 cup) dates
   (about 25–30 dates), pitted
150 g (5½ oz/¾ cup, lightly
   packed) brown sugar
150 g (5½ oz/1 cup)
   self-raising flour
150 g (5½ oz/1 cup)
   wholemeal self-raising flour
1 teaspoon bicarbonate of soda
   (baking soda)
175 g (6 oz/1½ cups)
   walnut halves
1 egg, lightly whisked

TO TRANSPORT
Wrap up the cooled loaf
in baking paper and string
for immediate delivery. The
good news is that it keeps
for ages (up to 7 days in
an airtight container in the
fridge) and also freezes well.

This can be put together in a large saucepan and requires no gadgets or machines, so just preheat your oven to 180°C (350°F) and get started. Line a large loaf tin (mine's about 29 x 10 cm/11½ x 4 in), or two smaller ones, with baking paper. If you are lucky enough to have, and brave enough to use, the traditional cylindrical nut-loaf tins, then go ahead and grease and line two of those.

Put your butter and 250 ml (9 fl oz/1 cup) of water in a large saucepan over medium heat and wait for the butter to melt. Now add the dates and stir to un-clump them. Add the sugar and stir to dissolve, then remove the pan from the heat.

Sift the two flours together. Then, with your sifted flours at the ready, add the bicarbonate of soda to the dates and stir as a lovely fizzing takes place. Quickly add the walnuts, then fold in the flours, followed by the egg.

Pour into the prepared tin(s) and bake for 40 minutes if you're making one large loaf, 30 minutes for smaller ones, or until a skewer inserted in the centre comes out clean.

Hot chocolate

Taking chocolates to cheer up a glum chum is very kind. But also a bit unoriginal, don't you think? If serious comfort is what's needed, a cup of home-made hot chocolate is like a perfectly timed, non-judgmental hug. Whizz up a jar of this stuff and take it to your forlorn friend; all they have to do (or you could do it, if it's beyond them in their current state) is mix it up.

As this isn't terribly sweet, it does double duty as a sensible, yet comforting drink in the morning. The spice element is also quite mild, so use the amounts here as a starting point for your own more potent blend, if you like your hot chocolate, well, hot. I often add ground cardamom to the mix.

Makes enough for
at least 10 drinks
50 g (1¾ oz) dark
    (70% cocoa) chocolate
40 g (1½ oz/⅓ cup)
    unsweetened cocoa powder
    – the best you can find
1½ tablespoons caster
    (superfine) sugar
1 teaspoon ground cinnamon
pinch of ground cloves
½ teaspoon ground ginger
scant grinding of
    black pepper

TO TRANSPORT
Transfer the hot chocolate mixture to a clean, dry jar and give to someone who needs a bit of cheering up or cheering on.

Grate or chop the chocolate into small pieces. Put it, along with all the other ingredients, in an electric spice grinder or the small bowl of a food processor and whizz for half a minute or so. There should be no trace of chocolate pieces left. (If you are making this on a hot day, give the chopped chocolate 5 minutes in the fridge before it goes in the processor.)

To make up the hot chocolate, dissolve a tablespoon of the mixture in a little boiling water, then top up with warm milk.

Breakfast bread-and-butter pudding

When my mum was growing up, her family would occasionally leave their Gawler Hills farm and head to Henley Beach in Adelaide for a holiday. While there, they subsisted almost entirely on grilled cheese, bacon and tomato on toast. For two generations now, such a dish has been synonymous with Sunday nights, holidays and other times when the rules of nutrition are hedonistically abandoned. I don't eat bacon these days, but the combination of bread, cheese and borderline-charred tomato still brings a familiar feeling of contentment. Here, these are regrouped as a savoury bread-and-butter pudding that is perfect for breakfast. It will puff up nicely in the oven and imbue the home of your lucky recipient with that unmistakeable toasted-gruyère smell. One day, someone clever will invent a room-spray of that smell and I will give them all my money.

Serves 4

3 tablespoons olive oil
1 tablespoon balsamic vinegar
1 tablespoon brown sugar
1 clove garlic, crushed
250 g (9 oz) cherry tomatoes,
    cut in half
1 x 30 cm (12 in) baguette,
    cut into 1 cm (½ in) slices
softened butter, for spreading
50 g (1¾ oz) pecorino or
    parmesan, finely grated
50 g (1¾ oz) gruyère, grated
50 g (1¾ oz) cheddar, grated
50 g (1¾ oz) mozzarella, grated
2 tablespoons basil pesto

SAVOURY CUSTARD
600 ml (21 fl oz) milk
½ onion, halved and peeled
2 fresh bay leaves
3 eggs, lightly beaten

TO TRANSPORT
As the bread will have soaked up the liquid, you just need a flat-based basket and a tea towel if you're not going far, or an Esky (cool box) if you're covering more ground.

Preheat the oven to 160°C (315°F). Whisk together the oil, balsamic vinegar, sugar and garlic in a large bowl to make a dressing, then add the tomatoes and toss to coat. Transfer the tomatoes to a baking dish, arranging them cut-side up. Spoon over any left-over dressing and season with salt and pepper. Now roast them in the oven for an hour, at the end of which they should be wilted, a bit shrivelly and nicely caramelised.

For the savoury custard, heat the milk in a small saucepan with the onion and bay leaves over low heat. Let it simmer for 5 minutes to infuse, then cover and allow to cool. Haul out the onion, bay leaves and any icky skin that has formed on the surface while your back was turned. Whisk in the eggs – now you have your custard. Season to taste with salt and white pepper, keeping in mind that you have lots of salty cheese coming up too.

Lightly butter your baguette slices. Butter a medium baking dish and sprinkle the inside with some of the parmesan. Combine all the cheeses. Place a layer of bread in the bottom of the dish, then sprinkle over a third of the cheese and a few roasted tomato halves. Add some dobs of pesto. Now add more bread, then more cheese, tomato and pesto, and so on, until you have filled the dish (but save some of the cheese to sprinkle on top before baking). Now slowly pour your custard over the top – it will take a while to soak in properly, so keep topping up until the bread has absorbed all it can. Chill the pudding in the fridge until you're ready to cook (or travel).

When ready to bake, sprinkle with cheese and consign to a preheated 180°C (350°F) oven for 30 minutes or until puffed and golden. Serve immediately – on cooling, 'proud and puffed' can all too quickly lapse into 'dank and rubbery'.

Drop-off breakfast

Sweet fruit breakfast focaccia

There are so many things to love about focaccia: it isn't difficult to make, it goes a long way, and because it is best within a few hours of being baked, there is every excuse for polishing off the whole tray in one go. This version was inspired by Tessa Kiros' brilliant strawberry focaccia recipe, here changed to accommodate late-summer stone fruit – and with the timing fiddled, so you can begin the night before.

Serves at least 8

310 ml (10¾ fl oz/1¼ cups) lukewarm water
2 teaspoons active dried yeast
55 g (2 oz/¼ cup) granulated sugar, plus 1 tablespoon extra for sprinkling
400 g (14 oz) strong white bread flour
pinch of fine salt
olive oil, for greasing
4 ripe nectarines (or other stone fruit), thinly sliced
icing (confectioners') sugar, for dusting

TO TRANSPORT
When your focaccia is cooked, cover the top with a sheet of baking paper then wrap it – still in its tin – in a clean tea towel to keep it warm. Speed off to your nearest friend (who, ideally, will also have a first-rate coffee machine) and dust with icing sugar on site.

Start the evening beforehand. Close to bedtime, pour the water into a large bowl and sprinkle the yeast and half of the sugar on the top. Sift in the flour and salt and stir until a loose dough forms. Now knead the dough for about 5 minutes. Don't bother with tipping it out onto the bench, just work the dough inside the bowl – it will save you some cleaning-up time. To the fridge with the dough, and *buona notte* to you.

First thing in the morning (and it needs to be at least 90 minutes before you want to eat, so up and at 'em), line a 30 x 20 cm (12 x 8 in) baking tray with baking paper and rub a generous amount of olive oil all over it. Now stretch out your dough to reach all corners of the tray and set aside.

Place the nectarines in a bowl with the remaining sugar and toss gently.

Return to your baking tray. The dough will have shrunk back a little, so re-train its edges back to the edges of the tray, then cover with a sheet of oiled plastic wrap and leave in a warm, cosy place for about an hour. Time enough to shower and – if you do not have small children in the house – flick through the newspaper.

Preheat the oven to 200°C (400°F). Because your dough is so spread out and flat, it won't look very much increased in size, but it will be a bit puffy. Arrange the nectarine slices in neat rows, using your fingers to flick some of the delicious sugary juices all over as you go, then sprinkle the extra sugar over the top. Bake for 20–25 minutes or until risen and golden. Dust with icing sugar to serve.

Drop-off breakfast

Date and banana mini-pancakes

These are pikelets really. What is the difference? Not all that much, I guess, though you really don't see the pikelet on menus at smart cafes too often these days. My Auntie Betty was a mad pikelet fan – they were her bring-along picnic offering of choice, and she tended to serve them cold and buttered. Wendy has a friend who hauls a big jug of pancake batter to other people's houses and makes little pancakes. He then flips them from the pan to waiting children like a zookeeper dishing out the pilchards in the seal pool. So, you see, the pancake can travel in all sorts of fond ways.

Since all the sweetness comes from the banana and dates in this recipe, these little snacks are, technically, sugar-free. Which probably makes them a health food.

Serves 4–6

2 or 3 very ripe,
   squishy bananas
5 dates, pitted and finely diced
200 g (7 oz/1⅓ cups) self-
   raising flour
2 eggs
200 ml (7 fl oz) milk – or use
   170 ml (5½ fl oz/⅔ cup)
   milk and 2 tablespoons
   plain yoghurt for extra rise
vegetable oil, for frying
butter, to serve

In a large bowl, smash the bananas into a sloppy mess, then sprinkle in the dates, mixing as you go. The main challenge here is to have the dates evenly distributed instead of clumped together. Now sift in the flour, alternating with the eggs and milk here and there, until you have one big bowl of lumpy batter.

Heat a lick of oil in a non-stick frying pan over medium heat. Drop tablespoonfuls of the batter into the pan: you should be able to cook 3 or 4 pancakes at a time. When the edges start to bubble, turn them over and cook for a minute on the other side: you are looking for a light to golden brown colour.

Serve with butter – and lashings of tea.

TO TRANSPORT
For an off-site breakfast, either pack up the cooked pancakes in an open-topped basket with your smartest, cleanest tea towel over the top. Or, if you know the person well enough, take the jug of batter along and elbow your way into the kitchen.

Breakfast calzone

The first time I ate calzone was in the late 1980s, with Wendy at Don Giovanni's, a late-night place on Rundle Street in Adelaide. The calzone was so enormous – about the size and dimensions of a sleeping pug dog – that the two of us could order one, start at either end, never meet in the middle, and still not have to eat for days. Student heaven. (Our other cheap-night-out trick was to donate blood, which in those days earned you a stubbie of Coopers Stout and a biscuit.)

There is an element of genius to calzone; a folded-over pizza that allows both for more topping and for the thrill of transportability. Granted, calzone is a bit of a stretch for inclusion in a chapter on breakfasts. But if you are the kind of person who likes pizza for late breakfast (guilty as charged) or a fry-up (yes, indeed), then keep an open mind on this. The filling here is a suggestion, but it could take whatever breakfast items you like, as long as they're not going to release too much water during cooking, or you will end up with a soggy base. Plan ahead: the dough needs to rest overnight before the calzones are cooked and then dropped off for reheating.

Makes 6

375 ml (13 fl oz/1½ cups)
   lukewarm water
2 teaspoons active dried yeast
2 teaspoons raw sugar
2 tablespoons olive oil, plus
   extra for drizzling and frying
500 g (1 lb 2 oz/3⅓ cups)
   strong white bread flour
½ teaspoon fine salt

FILLING

2 large brown onions
1 tablespoon thyme leaves
4 rainbow chard leaves,
   finely chopped
6 sun-dried tomatoes
12 button mushrooms, sliced
18 cherry tomatoes

TO TRANSPORT

Swathe your tray of calzones in a clean tea towel, then give them a quick blast in a hot oven at their destination.

Put the lukewarm water in a jug, mix in the yeast, sugar and olive oil and leave to stand for about 5–10 minutes to activate the yeast.

Mix the flour and salt in a large bowl, then form a well in the middle and pour in the yeast mixture. With a rubber spatula, slowly bring in the flour, mixing to form a dough. Cover and leave to rest for 10 minutes. Give the dough a light knead until it forms a nice smooth ball, then drizzle over some olive oil to coat it thinly. Cover the bowl and refrigerate overnight.

Next day, make the filling. Thinly slice the onions then, in a heavy-based frying pan over medium heat, fry them in a little olive oil until soft, stirring often. Turn down the heat to low and cook for another 15 minutes, or until they are totally collapsed and a bit jammy. Crumble in the thyme, then scrape the onion mix to one side of the pan. Add the chard to the pan and cook until it is just wilted. Stir in the remaining filling ingredients except the cherry tomatoes. Preheat the oven to its hottest setting, about 250°C (500°F), and line a large baking sheet with baking paper. Divide the dough into six even balls, then roll each one out into a circle about 20 cm (8 in) across. Place a sixth of the filling ingredients on half of each circle, put the tomatoes on top, then fold over to form a half-moon, or pasty, shape.

Place the calzones on the prepared baking sheet and bake for 10 minutes or until golden and cooked through.

Ruby gravadlax

This dish takes two days to make, but your patience will be rewarded with a delicate treat that is pretty as a picture. Try to snare a fillet from the middle part of the salmon, so you are dealing with a regular thickness. Any thinner parts will cure before the rest of the fish, and over-cured salmon can be weirdly dry. This recipe is for quite a modest amount, because I like to eat it within a few days.

Serves 2–4

250 g (9 oz) fillet of salmon, ideally centre-cut, skin off
1 teaspoon coriander seeds
1 teaspoon green peppercorns
80 g (2¾ oz) coarse salt
80 g (2¾ oz) granulated sugar
50 g (1¾ oz) raw beetroot, grated
1 tablespoon gin
1 x 20 g (¾ oz) bunch of dill, torn into 4 or 5 pieces

DILL AND
MUSTARD SAUCE
1½ tablespoons dijon mustard
1½ tablespoons wholegrain mustard
1 tablespoon runny honey
1 tablespoon white balsamic vinegar or cider vinegar
2 tablespoons extra virgin olive oil
1½ tablespoons finely chopped dill

Rinse your fish and pat it very dry with paper towel. Now, using a pestle and mortar, bash the coriander seeds and peppercorns until they are coarsely crushed, then stir in the salt, sugar, beetroot and gin. Rub this cure, along with the dill, all over both sides of your salmon. Lay the fish on a large piece of plastic wrap, placing a couple of the dill pieces underneath and the rest on top, then wrap it tightly. Put the salmon in a non-reactive (ceramic or glass) dish with a similar-sized plate or baking tray on top weighted down with something heavy, like an unopened bag of rice – or a few tins if you have a refrigerator that large. (The original Scandinavian fish-curers had no worries about fridge space, obviously; they just dug a hole in the garden and left the fish in there to cure.) Leave the fish for at least a day, but preferably 2 days, draining off any liquid twice a day, or whenever you think to do it.

The day before you plan to serve the gravadlax, make the dill and mustard sauce. Mix all the ingredients together, then transfer to a clean jar and refrigerate overnight to let the flavours develop. These amounts make more sauce than you need, but on account of its outrageous deliciousness, you'll probably find other uses for it – it will keep for up to 4 days in the fridge.

When you can wait no longer, unwrap the fish and discard the dill. Scrape off as much of the cure as you can, then give the salmon a very quick rinse under the tap. If too much of the cure is left on, the fish will be too salty; try not to get it too wet and waterlogged, though. Pat the fish dry with paper towel again and you are ready to go. I like gravadlax sliced very thinly, but that part is up to you.

TO TRANSPORT
Unless you are travelling by open snowmobile, you'll need to use an ice-pack to keep the pre-sliced gravadlax chilled. At your destination, twirl the slices on toast and serve with the sauce. Of course, gravadlax isn't just for breakfast; it's also good for lunch, dinner, and served on small toasts for canapés.

Corn fritters

Every Tom, Dick and his dog has a recipe for corn fritters these days. I accept that. And I blame Bill Granger, which I think is also fair. But if I can venture a suggestion, it would be this: add grated halloumi. And cumin. And lime. And lots of herbs, to turn your fritters into greeny-goldy, salty, crunchy little bundles. This mix is very light on the batter and hence not doughy in the slightest, but more like a rosti. Serve it for breakfast, with a little salsa made of diced avocado and tomato, a squirt of lime juice, some olive oil and more coriander. If you absolutely must have some sort of porcine-derived product along for the ride, you could add a few strips of oven-crisped pancetta. But that would be overdoing it, in my opinion. One other note: this recipe also works quite nicely with gluten-free flour. Just saying.

Makes 24 small fritters,
or 12 larger ones

3 ears sweetcorn, kernels sliced
   from the cobs
1 small red onion, thinly sliced
100 g (3½ oz) halloumi,
   coarsely grated
75 g (2½ oz/½ cup) plain
   (all-purpose) flour –
   or gluten-free flour
½ teaspoon baking powder
1 teaspoon cumin seeds,
   toasted in a dry pan then
   ground into a powder
handful of coriander (cilantro)
   leaves, roughly chopped
small handful of dill
   fronds, chopped
finely grated zest of 1 lime
juice of ½ lime
3 eggs, separated
vegetable oil, for frying

In a large bowl, mix the corn kernels with the onion, halloumi, flour, baking powder, cumin and herbs. Add the lime zest and juice, along with the egg yolks, and stir through until the whole thing is chunkily combined.

In another bowl, whisk your egg whites to soft peaks. Add a third of the egg whites to the corn mixture and stir through to loosen, then gently fold in the rest of the egg whites.

Heat a 1 cm (½ in) depth of oil in a large heavy-based frying pan until it's hazy. Drop heaped tablespoonfuls of the batter into the hot oil, taking care to flatten the fritters a bit and guide any stray kernels back to home base; for larger fritters, aim for about 80 ml (⅓ cup) of batter for each one, flattening it out to a diameter of about 10 cm (4 in). (The edges will be ragged. It's fine. Think of this as an opportunity for salty cheese to meet oil. Don't resist it.)

Cook for about 3 minutes on each side or until golden and cooked through, then drain well on paper towel. Keep warm in a 120°C (235°F) oven until you're ready to serve.

TO TRANSPORT
These are delicious straight from the pan, of course, but will work equally well cold after a journey in a tin or container, interleaved with sheets of paper towel. Smaller fritters can be handed round at picnics or cocktail parties too. If you have any fritters left over, cut them into slices and toss through a rocket (arugula) salad dressed with vinaigrette. Yum.

Quince tea jelly

Perfect on hot buttered toast for breakfast, or as an impromptu glaze for fruit tartlets (see page 142), this quince jelly has a trace of spiced tea – an idea borrowed from the splendid Parisian tea merchants Mariage Freres, who infuse apple jelly with their exquisite teas. If you're lucky enough to have a quince tree in your backyard, you never really know how many quinces you are going to get, so this is an old-fashioned proportional recipe. Dust off that part of your brain that does maths and work out the quantity of sugar to match the yield of juice from your quince harvest (or make the sums a homework exercise for the nearest child . . .).

Makes 2 litres (35 fl oz/8 cups)
about 3 kg (6 lb 12 oz)
 ripe quinces
about 2 kg (4 lb 8 oz)
 granulated sugar
small teacup of brewed spiced
 tea, such as black chai

STERILISING JARS OR BOTTLES
My preferred method is a hot wash (ideally in a dishwasher) followed by 10 minutes in a 140°C (280°F) oven.

TO TRANSPORT
Label and date your jelly. If you can't resist a bit of zhushing, tie a square of cloth and a swing tag around the neck of each jar. Unopened jars of quince jelly will keep for a year in a cool, dark place; after opening, they should be refrigerated and used up in a couple of months.

Rub the quinces to remove their downy fluff. (Better still, have some small children take care of this.) Wash the quince and cut into 2 cm (¾ in) cubes, leaving the skin, pips, everything; only bother with removing the stalks and any black gritty bits. Put the fruit in a heavy-based stockpot or large saucepan, add just enough water to cover and simmer until very soft – this could take anywhere between 1 and 2 hours. Now drain the quince and take to it with a potato masher until you have a slushy mix with most big lumps gone.

Transfer the quince mush to a very fine sieve or a colander lined with muslin (cheesecloth) – I once used a pair of cheap low-denier tights stretched over a bowl and it worked surprisingly well. Squeeze to extract as much juice as possible. Don't worry about this making the jelly cloudy; I've discovered that any fine pulp that creeps through obligingly rises to the top as the jelly cooks and can be skimmed off. Now weigh the juice and measure out ⅚ of this weight of sugar (it's okay, you can use a calculator).

Place a couple of saucers in the freezer to chill – these are for testing the set of the jelly later. Add the tea to the bowl of quince juice, then tip back into the pot, along with the sugar. Simmer (and skim) for about 10 minutes or until the jelly turns a nice pink or ruby colour. When it starts to look a bit viscous, take a saucer from the freezer and place a drop of jelly on it: if it forms a droplet with a slightly wrinkly skin, you are good to go; if not, keep cooking for another few minutes and test again. Use a ladle to transfer the hot jelly to hot sterilised jars – be jolly careful, this stuff will really burn. Screw on the lids and admire your handiwork.

Pink grapefruit salad

If, like me, you are interested in food but also bone idle, I can thoroughly recommend having an energetic childhood friend who moves to France for a bit. *Voilà*! You can enjoy all the epiphanic food moments, with none of the swollen ankles and administrative tedium of international travel. Wendy is mad for a place called Le Vieux Logis, in the village of Trémolat, where apparently there's always something on the menu that pairs grapefruit with tarragon, a combination I would never ordinarily have stumbled across outside my routine composting activities. This salad is her adaptation . . . and it is beyond delicious, with a note of rosewater. And pretty as a picture, of course. Use the finer-leaved French tarragon here, or if all that aniseed freaks you out, you could substitute mint – always a winner.

Serves 4

2 pink grapefruit
about ½ teaspoon rosewater
½ teaspoon caster
   (superfine) sugar
1 teaspoon tarragon leaves

TO TRANSPORT
In a jar, of course, to show off the pretty pink of the grapefruit. This salad also looks lovely with different-coloured citrus fruit, but I have found that not all citrus (looking at you, yellow grapefruit) pairs as well with the rosewater.

The path to beautiful, jewel-like segments of pink grapefruit begins with an inordinately sharp knife. Using the knife, remove the peel, cutting deep enough to remove not only peel but pith too. You will now be holding a lovely pink sphere marked longitudinally with thin lines of white membrane, somewhat reminiscent of those chocolate oranges people used to give each other at Christmas before they started to give each other panettone instead (we have a dry-stone wall of these in our cupboard).

Holding the grapefruit over a bowl to catch the juice, use your el-sharpo knife to slice decisively through to the core on either side of each of these lines, cutting out the flesh in a wedge and leaving the membrane behind. When you've finished, you can squeeze the sad little membrane-concertina you're left with of its residual juice, then bin – or compost – it. Add the rosewater and sugar to the bowl of grapefruit segments, stirring to dissolve the sugar. (The potency of rosewater varies enormously between brands, so add a few drops at a time until it tastes right.)

Artfully arrange your grapefruit salad in a shallow dish, pour over the juice and sprinkle with the tarragon leaves.

Lunch

Tartines

Right. You know when you're calling round to somebody's place – maybe it's to discuss something in particular, or to collect something, or to shame-facedly return their power drill you borrowed eighteen months ago? Well, how about swinging by the bakery on the way, buying a nice loaf of high-end bread, and taking your own custom-built spread? In a jar, obviously, seeing as things need to be in jars to be taken seriously these days.

Just between ourselves, we can admit that this concept is not a million miles from the 'open-faced sandwich' that has plagued working lunches ever since the pocket protector was invented. But, at the Poilane café in Paris, they call open sandwiches 'tartines', and people pay 10 euros for them, so I think let's call them tartines. Yes? So, turn up with your jar and your loaf. Then, all you need to do is toast slices, and pile whatever you have on top. The following toppings are the product of various fever dreams had by Wendy and me over the years. The mackerel, umeboshi, radish and edamame one is freakishly good – I'm just going to say it. The roasted grapes are borrowed from a recipe in Peter Gordon's brilliant *Salads* book. And the coronation lentils are from when Wendy, living in London as a vegetarian, felt intense food jealousy at her first job where everyone else ate coronation chicken baps for lunch. The white bean spread is included because there can never be enough white beans.

Coronation lentils tartine

Serves 4

1½ tablespoons mayonnaise
1½ tablespoons crème fraîche
  or sour cream
1½ teaspoons curry powder
3 hard-boiled eggs
¼ tart green or crisp red apple,
  cut into matchsticks
about 1 tablespoon chopped
  coriander (cilantro), plus
  extra to garnish
3 tablespoons cooked Puy-
  style lentils – tinned are fine
slices of toasted sourdough,
  to serve

In a medium bowl, combine the mayo, crème fraîche or sour cream and curry powder.

Peel and roughly chop the hard-boiled eggs. Add to the bowl, along with all the remaining ingredients except the toast, then gently fold everything together.

To serve, pile on top of toast and finish with a little extra coriander and a grinding of pepper.

Recipes continued overleaf . . .

Pumpkin, roasted grape and goat's cheese tartine

Serves 4

300 g (10½ oz) pumpkin,
    peeled and cut into 2 cm
    (¾ in) cubes
olive oil, for drizzling
150 g (5½ oz) seedless
    red grapes
1 tablespoon
    pomegranate molasses
1 teaspoon soy sauce
handful of rocket (arugula)
100 g (3½ oz) rindless
    soft goat's cheese or curd
slices of toasted sourdough,
    to serve

Preheat the oven to 180°C (350°F). Toss the pumpkin cubes in some olive oil, then spread out in a single layer on a baking tray and season with salt.

Scatter the grapes over another baking tray, then pour over the pomegranate molasses and soy sauce and a tablespoon or so of olive oil.

Roast both the pumpkin and the grapes for 15 minutes, giving the grapes a stir halfway through and scraping up any molasses that is starting to caramelise on the baking tray. If the pumpkin isn't completely soft after 15 minutes, give it a little longer. Leave both to cool, and then combine with the rocket.

To serve, gently squash some goat's cheese onto the toast and pile the pumpkin and grape mixture on top.

Mackerel, edamame and umeboshi tartine

Serves 4

50 g (1¾ oz) podded
    frozen edamame
2 red radishes, very thinly sliced
2 umeboshi plums,
    finely chopped
150 g (5½ oz) smoked
    mackerel, flaked
1 tablespoon coriander
    (cilantro) leaves
olive oil, for drizzling
slices of toasted sourdough,
    to serve

Put the edamame in a heatproof bowl and pour over a copious amount of boiling water. Leave for 1 minute, then drain and refresh under cold running water.

Tip the edamame into a medium bowl and add the radish, umeboshi, mackerel, coriander and just a dash of olive oil. Combine everything very, very gently. The fish is already quite oily and the umeboshi are astringent, so this doesn't need lemon juice or any other dressing.

To serve, pile on top of toast and finish with a grinding of pepper.

A NOTE ON INGREDIENTS
You should be able to find edamame (green soy beans) and umeboshi (salted plums) – make sure you get the mouth-puckeringly tart variety, rather than sweet ones – at Asian supermarkets. Substitute the mackerel with hot-smoked salmon, if push comes to shove.

White bean and roasted tomato tartine

Serves 4

200 g (7 oz) truss
    cherry tomatoes
olive oil, for drizzling
1 leek, well washed and outer
    green leaves discarded,
    finely chopped
1 clove garlic, finely chopped
about 2½ tablespoons
    white wine
1 x 400 g (14 oz) tin cannellini
    beans, rinsed and drained
50 g (1¾ oz/½ cup) finely
    grated parmesan
1 tablespoon tarragon or basil
    leaves, torn into small pieces
slices of toasted sourdough,
    to serve

Preheat the oven to 150°C (300°F). Place the tomatoes on a baking tray, drizzle generously with olive oil and season with salt. Roast for 20 minutes, or until nicely squishy but still holding their shape.

Meanwhile, pour a little olive oil into a heavy-based saucepan and place over medium heat. Add the leek and sauté for 2–3 minutes or until soft with a few brown bits, then add the garlic and sauté for another minute. Add the white wine and cannellini beans and let it bubble away for a couple of minutes. There should still be some moisture at the end of the cooking time, so add a tiny splash more wine if you need to. Remove from the heat and leave to cool until it is just warm.

Take out about half the beans and use a stick blender (or the small bowl of a food processor) to whizz them to a purée. Squash most of the rest of the beans into a rough mash with a fork, then return the bean purée to the pan, along with a pinch of salt, the parmesan and the herbs. Stir everything together. The mixture will thicken as it cools, so loosen with a little more olive oil, if you like.

To serve, spread a generous amount of the bean mash onto toast and plonk a couple of the roasted tomatoes on top.

Pea and tofu velvet soup

Oi! Stop! If you were about to keep flipping, thinking, 'Yeah, right. Tofu soup. Next!', then I implore you – not so fast. This soup combines freshness with vivid colour and a terrific, velvety smoothness that comes to you courtesy of silken tofu. You will need a powerful food processor or high-speed blender for best results here; I have achieved an acceptable consistency with a stick blender, but it did take some patience. This beautiful soup is delicious served warm in shallow bowls (perhaps with a few hot peppered scallops in the centre as an extra treat), chilled as a refreshing starter on a hot day, or in shot glasses at a drinks party. Enjoy it soon after it's made, though – this is one soup that doesn't take well to freezing.

Serves 6 as a starter

1 tablespoon butter
1 brown or white onion,
    finely chopped
200 g (7 oz) frozen peas
about 5 mint sprigs
800 ml (28 fl oz) light
    vegetable or chicken stock
150 g (5½ oz) silken tofu,
    roughly diced

TO TRANSPORT
Deliver the soup to your destination in a clear vessel, so the beautiful colour can be admired from all angles. If it is a party you are going to, gather as many little shot glasses as you have and carefully pour from your jug on-site. A grinding of pepper on top should seal the deal.

Melt the butter in a large saucepan over low–medium heat, then add the onion and cook gently until soft and becoming translucent – turn the heat down to low if you suspect the onion is even thinking about turning brown. Now add the peas, mint and stock and bring to the boil. As soon as the soup reaches boiling point, turn down the heat, put the lid on, and leave on the lowest-possible heat to simmer for 10 minutes. It's important to cook this at a gentle simmer, rather than a vigorous boil, or you'll end up with a more old-fashioned, mushy-pea taste. Such careful treatment also preserves some of the freshness of the peas and mint.

Remove the soup from the heat, add the tofu and leave for approximately 5 minutes to cool slightly. Now fish out the mint sprigs. It won't matter if you miss one or two, but now they've contributed their lovely flavour, the idea is to take them out so they won't turn the soup a sludgy colour.

Transfer the soup to a powerful food processor or blender (possibly in batches, depending on the size of your machine) and blitz it to as smooth a consistency as possible. You can serve this soup as is, or, for extra finesse, pass it through a sieve to take out any remaining pea skins.

Winter's consolation soup

This soup traces its origins to the most French of all dishes – *pot au feu*, or 'pot on the fire'. Usually this involves boiled beef and other meats, and several courses from the one pot: first, the bone marrow on toast; then the broth; and finally the meat and vegetables, served with an array of sharp accompaniments. This version skips all the meat and cuts straight to a hot broth with hefty chunks of vegetables and persillade, a zingy green mustard sauce. And makes winter almost worthwhile.

Serves 4

3 large carrots, peeled and
   cut into 5 cm (2 in) chunks
3 potatoes, peeled and cut
   into 5 cm (2 in) chunks
1 turnip, peeled and cut into
   4 cm (1½ in) chunks
2 leeks, well washed and outer
   green layers discarded, then
   cut into 5 cm (2 in) lengths
1 stalk celery, cut into 2 cm
   (¾ in) slices on the diagonal
1 thyme sprig
1 bay leaf
a few peppercorns
750 ml (26 fl oz/3 cups)
   good-quality stock
1 tablespoon olive oil

PERSILLADE
50 g (1¾ oz) flat-leaf parsley
2 cloves garlic
a few walnuts – optional
1 tablespoon chopped
   tarragon – optional
2 teaspoons dijon mustard
1 tablespoon lemon juice
pinch of sea salt
2 tablespoons olive oil

Put all the vegetables and the thyme, bay leaf and peppercorns into a big heavy saucepan or stockpot, then pour in the stock. Bring to the boil and let it bubble for a minute or so, then reduce the heat to low, cover and simmer for about 20 minutes.

While your soup is bubbling away, turn your attention to the persillade. Finely chop the parsley with the garlic and walnuts, if using. Transfer to a small bowl, then stir in the tarragon, if using, the mustard, lemon juice, salt and olive oil.

Check your vegetables – they should be nice and soft but still holding their shape. When they are at this stage, fish out the thyme, bay leaf and peppercorns and splash in the olive oil. Don't stir the soup too much, as it is nice to keep all the vegetables in their original shape.

To serve, ladle generous servings of vegetables and broth into shallow bowls and dollop a tablespoonful of persillade (or more) on top. I advise against stirring it into the soup, as it's so much nicer to watch it melt and deliberately scoop up little bits of it with each spoonful of soup.

TO TRANSPORT
A big jar or a well-sealed plastic container (there is no thickness to the broth, so it will splash about everywhere, given half a chance). The persillade should travel separately in its own small bowl or jar. If your recipient really looks like they need beefing up, slip half a tin of cooked and rinsed white beans or chickpeas into the pot a minute before the vegetables are cooked. This may not be traditional, but then neither is skipping the bone marrow.

Asian pumpkin and sweet potato soup with coriander nut pesto

This soup is what your Jewish mother would make for you when you had a cold… if she were Asian and confused, that is. Stepping out of the wreckage of that metaphor, I simply make the point that this dish has many of the attributes – sinus-clearing spiciness, tang and vitamin C from the lime, sweetness from the coconut milk and sweet potato, and the salty hit of fish sauce – that bring comfort to the afflicted, especially when a bowl is consumed in front of something awful on the television.

Serves 4

1 onion, finely chopped
vegetable oil, for frying
about 2 teaspoons Thai
   red curry paste
500 g (1 lb 2 oz) pumpkin,
   peeled and cut into 3 cm
   (1¼ in) cubes
1 sweet potato, peeled and
   cut into 3 cm (1¼ in) cubes
2 kaffir lime leaves, shredded
2 tablespoons red
   lentils – optional
1 teaspoon vegetable stock
   powder or ½ stock cube
200 ml (7 fl oz) coconut milk
1 scant teaspoon fish sauce

CORIANDER NUT PESTO
40 g (1½ oz) coriander
   (cilantro), leaves and stalks
40 g (1½ oz) almonds or
   cashews, or a mix of both
juice of 1 lime

In a large heavy-based saucepan, fry the onion in a glug of oil over medium heat until soft. Add the curry paste, reduce the heat to low and stir for a minute or so until aromatic. The heat level of curry pastes varies widely, so use your best judgement – if you like things really hot, go crazy with more.

Now throw in the pumpkin, sweet potato, lime leaves, lentils and 500 ml (17 fl oz/2 cups) of water. (The lentils are really only there to help create a nice smooth texture, so don't worry if you don't have them.) Bring to the boil, then reduce the heat to a gentle simmer and cook for 20 minutes or until the vegetables are soft. Stir in the stock powder or cube, then leave the soup to cool for a few minutes before blending to a perfectly smooth puree. Now stir through the coconut milk and fish sauce.

To make the pesto, whizz up the coriander and nuts in a mini food processor (or take a large cook's knife and chop like a demon). Some like this pesto smooth. I like it chunky. Add three-quarters of the lime juice, then taste and add more until the pesto has just the right amount of zing.

Gently reheat the soup if needed, then ladle into bowls and add a teaspoon of pesto to each one.

TO TRANSPORT
Take the soup in a large screw-top jar and the pesto in a smaller one. I know it isn't nice to be prescriptive with your gifts, but if it were up to me, I'd insist that the pesto be eaten incrementally with each spoonful of soup, rather than being swirled through it.

Zucchini and parmesan soup

Any soup with cheese in it is by definition comfort food. My friend Alice Ryan was the first person to casually let slip to me the electrifying advice that a pot of simmering minestrone is immeasurably enhanced by the addition of a spent parmesan rind. And I remember Wendy making zucchini and parmesan soup for me in the 1990s. The combination of zucchini with such a defiant amount of mustard, given sharpness and umami by the parmesan, is simple but striking. It's also very creamy in consistency. Look, while I wouldn't say this is a light soup, it's outrageously comforting, especially given its ideal serving companions of bread and butter, crème fraîche and as much parmesan as you can get away with.

The daftest cheese-containing soup I ever made was a pumpkin, cheddar and ale thing at which I fancied myself a dab hand at Uni. I left a pot of it out one night and by morning it was a vile, almost-sentient creature with clear plans to kill me and my housemates in our beds. So yeah – cheesy soup. It's great. Just don't turn your back on it.

Serves 4–6

2 onions, finely chopped
2 tablespoons butter,
    for frying
3 large potatoes – about
    360 g (12¾ oz) in total –
    peeled and cut into 1 cm
    (½ in) cubes
750 ml (26 fl oz/3 cups)
    vegetable stock
4 zucchini (courgettes),
    cut into 2 cm (¾ in) cubes
20 g (¾ oz) flat-leaf parsley,
    finely chopped, plus extra
    to serve
50 g (1¾ oz) parmesan, finely
    grated, plus extra to serve
1 tablespoon dijon mustard,
    or more to taste
crème fraîche or sour cream
    and buttered bread, to serve

In a large heavy-based saucepan or stockpot, fry the onions in the butter over low heat until they are translucent. Take care that your butter doesn't burn. Add the potatoes to the pan, then pour in the stock and bring to the boil. Add the zucchini, then reduce the heat to very low, cover and simmer gently for 15 minutes. Add the parsley and simmer for 5 minutes.

Make sure your vegetables are good and soft, then blitz half the soup with a stick blender until smooth (or blend in an upright blender). Return the blended soup to the pan and gently reheat if needed, then stir through the parmesan and mustard.

Serve with extra chopped parsley, even more parmesan, crème fraîche or sour cream and thickly buttered bread.

___

TO TRANSPORT
Carry in a large, well-sealed container. As you will have gathered, this is not a light soup, so think carefully before taking it to a convalescent.

Harira soup

Traditionally, this soup has lamb in it and is eaten to break the Ramadan fast. But as a vegetarian dish it's filling, virtuous and perfect for anyone convalescing or plagued by a cold or the flu.

Serves 4–6

1½ tablespoons olive oil
2 onions, coarsely chopped
3 stalks celery,
  coarsely chopped
3 large carrots,
  coarsely chopped
1 small fennel bulb,
  coarsely chopped
2 teaspoons ground cumin
1 teaspoon ground cinnamon
½ teaspoon ground turmeric
pinch of fennel seeds
5–6 saffron strands
2 tablespoons tomato paste
  (concentrated purée)
1 x 400 g (14 oz) tin tomatoes
1 x 400 g (14 oz) tin chickpeas,
  rinsed and drained
2 tablespoons red
  lentils, rinsed
750 ml (26 fl oz/3 cups) light
  vegetable stock
2 cloves garlic
1 cm (½ in) ginger
50 g (1¾ oz) flat-leaf parsley
  leaves and tender parts
  of the stems
30 g (1 oz) coriander (cilantro)
  leaves and tender stems
extra virgin olive oil or butter,
  dried mint and lemon
  wedges, to serve

Pour the olive oil into a large heavy-based saucepan and place over medium heat. Add the onion and cook until soft and translucent. Now add the celery, carrot and fennel and cook for a few minutes until starting to soften. Stir in the cumin, cinnamon, turmeric, fennel seeds and saffron and cook, stirring, for a few seconds until aromatic. Next, give the tomato paste a twirl around the pan for 2 minutes, then add the tomatoes and all their juice. (Speaking of tomatoes, there has been a trend of late towards pre-chopped or crushed tinned tomatoes, but can I urge you to reconsider the old-fashioned whole peeled tomato? I find that they taste better, and you are less likely to end up with mush.) Now add the chickpeas, lentils and stock. Bring to the boil, then reduce the heat to a low simmer and cook, covered, for about 20 minutes.

While the soup is cooking, take your biggest chopping board and really go for it with a large cook's knife until the garlic, ginger and fresh herbs are chopped to a fine paste. Stir this through the soup about 5 minutes before the end of the cooking time, breaking up the whole tomatoes with the back of a spoon as you go.

One of the tricks when making a meatless version of a meat soup is to add an extra glug of olive oil or a dab of butter to help carry the other flavours in the soup and make it altogether more satisfying. So do this, then sprinkle very lightly with dried mint and serve with lemon wedges on the side.

A NOTE ON RAS EL HANOUT
If you are the type of person who presses 'I'm feeling lucky' on internet search engines, you might like to skip the mix of spices suggested here and head straight for a high-quality ras el hanout. This is a North African spice blend, of which there are about as many versions as there are people who make it. It is a good shortcut for cooks in a hurry, but do augment it with some saffron.

TO TRANSPORT
Carry the soup in a tightly sealed receptacle. Pack a small sachet of mint and a lemon separately.

Lemon thyme Niçoise salad

I think the Niçoise is just about my favourite salad-as-meal. When Wendy and I lived in London, the two of us and our mate Jo Fox missed Sirena tinned tuna in chilli oil so much we would demand that any visiting Australians carry demented amounts of it in their luggage. (Obviously, smuggling-wise, it's not as bad as king parrots down your trousers or anything, but it's still slightly weird, I accept.) Anyway, a lot of Niçoise was made. This one uses fresh tuna, though, crusted on the outside with sesame and lemon thyme.

Serves 4

40 g (1½ oz/¼ cup) sesame seeds
½ teaspoon ground cumin
1 teaspoon finely chopped lemon thyme
1 x 500 g (1 lb 2 oz) piece sashimi-grade tuna
olive oil, for frying and marinating
2 tablespoons salted capers
1 clove garlic, crushed with the flat of a heavy knife
12 baby potatoes, cut in half
250 g (9 oz) green beans, topped and tailed
250 g (9 oz) cherry tomatoes, cut in half
4 hard-boiled eggs, peeled and cut into wedges
80 g (2¾ oz/½ cup) black or kalamata olives, cut in half and pitted

LEMON THYME DRESSING
80 ml (2½ fl oz/⅓ cup) olive oil
juice of 1 large lemon
1 teaspoon dijon mustard
1 teaspoon honey
2 tablespoons lemon thyme, chopped and bruised

Tip the sesame seeds, cumin and lemon thyme onto a plate with a grinding of salt and pepper. Roll the tuna in this mixture to coat, pressing on the seeds. Heat a thin film of oil in a frying pan and sear the tuna for a minute on each side, then set aside to rest. (I like my tuna very rare, but you can cook it for longer, of course.)

Now, soak the salted capers in water for 5 minutes, so they'll be marginally less salty. Pat dry, then leave to marinate in a tablespoon of olive oil with the garlic clove while you make the rest of the salad.

Time for the rest of the salad. Boil the potatoes until tender. Steam the green beans until just tender, then refresh under the cold tap and drain.

Now – back to those capers. Heat a small frying pan over high heat, haul out the garlic clove and tip in the capers and oil. They should frazzle nicely. Stir until the capers are crisp, then remove with a slotted spoon.

Whisk the dressing ingredients together, season well with salt flakes and freshly ground black pepper and pour over the warm potatoes. Add everything else except the tuna and capers and toss gently. Transfer the salad to a serving plate or platter. Cut the tuna into 5 mm (¼ in) slices and arrange over the salad, then finish with the crispy capers.

TO TRANSPORT
If you are travelling with this salad, take the cooled seared tuna in plastic wrap. Pack the dressed potatoes in one container and the eggs, olives, tomatoes and beans in another, then when you get to your destination, toss them all together and pile on a plate. Whip out your tuna and – with a sharp knife – cut it into 5 mm (¼ in) slices. You should have something exceedingly pretty. Arrange the slices on and in the salad, scatter with the crispy capers and serve.

French lentil salad

The key to the success of this salad is the type of lentil you use, and for many years there was only one candidate for the job: the Puy lentil, grown in the volcanic soils of France's Auvergne region. A pretty, speckled little thing, it is not guilty of any of the crimes of which lentils are commonly accused, namely sludginess and blandness. However, it is with a little gust of national pride that I announce the arrival of an Australian-grown lentil that's equal to the task – look for small greenish 'French-style' or 'Puy-style' lentils and you can't go wrong. Serve this salad with just about anything: gratins, tarts or quiches, smoked or roast salmon, a poached egg, a slice of toast slathered with goat's cheese, or just a glass of red wine. If you are meat-minded, feel free to add sautéed lardons.

Serves 4–6

210 g (7½ oz/1 cup)
    Puy-style lentils
1 star anise or clove
½ large onion, peeled
    but left intact
½ fennel bulb – or just use
    2 more stalks celery
1 carrot, peeled
2 cloves garlic, halved and any
    green shoots removed
2 bay leaves
1 rosemary sprig
2 large pieces dried
    porcini – optional
2 tablespoons chopped
    flat-leaf parsley
2 stalks celery, finely diced

VINAIGRETTE

1 teaspoon dijon mustard
juice of ½ lemon
3 tablespoons olive oil
2 spring onions (scallions),
    finely chopped

TO TRANSPORT
This salad is fine to dress in advance, so stir through the vinaigrette, decant to a receptacle with a tight-fitting lid and deliver.

Rinse the lentils under a fast-running tap, picking out any un-lentil-like bits you come across. If you have time, leave the lentils to soak in cold water for about half an hour, then drain. But if you are not the plan-ahead type, here's a short cut. Tip the washed lentils into a medium saucepan, cover with cold water and bring to the boil, then cook for 1 minute before draining and rinsing again. Push the star anise or clove into the onion half, so it will be easier to fish out later. Place the soaked or pre-cooked lentils in the rinsed-out saucepan, along with all the remaining ingredients except the parsley and celery. Bring to the boil, then simmer for about 30 minutes.

Use the lentil-cooking time to make the vinaigrette. Sprinkle a little salt and pepper in the bottom of a bowl and add the mustard and lemon juice. Squash with the back of a teaspoon, then stir until combined. Slowly dribble in the olive oil, stirring all the while, and you should end up with something lovely, shiny and smooth. Stir in the spring onion and set aside.

Check the lentils for doneness by sinking your teeth into one – it should be tender, but still have a little bit of firmness. When the lentils are ready, drain them (but keep the liquid – see note below), removing the vegetables and herbs. While the lentils are still hot, stir through the vinaigrette, parsley and celery.

A NOTE ON LENTIL STOCK
Don't waste the lentil-cooking liquid. Just sieve out all the 'extras' before freezing the stock for up to 3 months, ready for adding body and flavour to your next pearl barley and lentil orzotto (see page 91) or spaghetti lentilaise (see page 86). I like to chop the vegetables salvaged from the stock and polish them off with a bit of the broth, some butter and salt – a perk of the job.

Fattoush

The first best thing about fattoush, the fabulous Lebanese salad in which pitta bread is royally primped with herbs and lettuce, is saying the word 'fattoush'. It is an extremely pleasing word to utter. A perfect partner for grilled fish or prawns, or fried halloumi, this terrific salad is colourful and crunchy – and all its healthy salad-y bits allow one to overlook the fact that one is in it mainly for the croûtons. Wendy, knowing my fondness for peach in a salad, once boldly chopped one into a fattoush, and the results were pretty great. This recipe is endlessly adaptable and could also take the addition of finely chopped celery and some avocado. If you have purists coming for lunch, just swap the peach for tomato and leave out the coriander.

Serves 6–8

2 round pitta breads
1 tablespoon olive oil
½ iceberg lettuce
20 cm (8 in) length cucumber
1 ripe peach, peeled and cut
    into 2 cm (¾ in) pieces
4 red radishes, finely sliced
large handful of flat-leaf
    parsley, finely chopped
large handful of coriander
    (cilantro), finely chopped
2 tablespoons shredded
    mint leaves
2 tablespoons chopped
    dill – optional
1 tablespoon sumac
YOGHURT DRESSING
2 tablespoons olive oil
3 tablespoons lemon juice
1 tablespoon plain yoghurt
2 spring onions (scallions),
    finely sliced

Start with the pitta bread. Preheat the oven to 180°C (350°F). Rub olive oil over both sides of the bread, then cut into rough 2 cm (¾ in) squares. Sprinkle with salt and bake for about 5 minutes or until crispy, then set aside to cool.

Next make the dressing. Whisk together the olive oil, lemon juice and yoghurt with a pinch of salt until well combined, then stir through the spring onion.

Separate the lettuce leaves and chop into roughly 2 cm (¾ in) pieces. Now cut the cucumber in half lengthways and run a teaspoon down the centre to scoop out the seeds (either add these seeds, with some mint leaves, to a long gin and tonic, or discard), then slice on the diagonal to make nice long curves. Put the lettuce and cucumber in a large bowl and add the peach, radish, all the herbs and half the sumac. Pour in the dressing and gently toss everything together. Sprinkle over the crispy pitta and the rest of the sumac – and perhaps another drizzle of olive oil, because a salad just doesn't seem complete without it.

TO TRANSPORT
Take the salad and crispy pitta separately and dress on-site about 10 minutes before serving.

Winter tabbouleh

This tabbouleh is bulked up for winter with chickpeas and, as such, is *not* a traditional version. But it's a good excuse to eat fennel, and it's beautifully colourful even when the sky isn't. Yes, there are a lot of herbs here – but it is, after all, a herb salad. If you are one of those who prefers mostly bulgur in their tabbouleh, then you could tone down the parsley a little bit.

This very portable salad is also cheered up with a good zesty dressing. You can convert it into a very satisfying meal by adding grilled halloumi and warmed pitta bread, though you must remember to grill your halloumi on-site to avoid the 'Am I eating a cold thong?' texture of halloumi that's been cooked and cooled.

Serves 4–6

100 g (3½ oz) fine
 bulgur (burghul)
about 500 ml (17 fl oz/2 cups)
 boiling water
1 red onion, finely chopped
olive oil, for frying
½ teaspoon ground cumin
2 teaspoons red wine vinegar
150 g (5½ oz) flat-leaf parsley
50 g (1¾ oz)
 coriander (cilantro)
30 g (1 oz) mint
1 x 400 g (14 oz) tin chickpeas,
 rinsed and drained
1 small bulb fennel, shaved
seeds from ½ pomegranate –
 about 150 g (5½ oz)

POMEGRANATE
DRESSING
1 clove garlic, very
 finely chopped
1 tablespoon
 pomegranate molasses
½ teaspoon ground cinnamon
2 tablespoons olive oil

First, combine all the dressing ingredients in a small jar, screw on the lid and give it a good shake, then set aside.

Now rinse the bulgur in a sieve under plenty of running water, then tip into a bowl. Pour over the boiling water and leave to soak for 5 minutes. Drain off the excess water, then leave to cool.

In a heavy-based frying pan, fry the onion in a little olive oil over medium heat until just starting to soften. Add the cumin and cook, stirring, for 2 minutes, then remove from the heat and stir in the vinegar.

Rinse all the herbs and remove the stems from the mint, then get busy with a cook's knife and chop them all into a green mess with no large pieces left.

In a large bowl, combine the cooled bulgur with the onion mixture, the chickpeas and the chopped herbs.

About 10 minutes before serving, add the dressing and stir well to combine. Finish with the fennel and pomegranate seeds.

TO TRANSPORT
Travel with the main salad in one bowl, the dressing in a little jar, and the fennel and pomegranate seeds in their own separate container.

Barbecued eggplant smash with pitta crisps

This is a proper barbecue-stopper. Sure, I hear you say, but it's only a variation on baba ganoush. Not so fast – this is chunkier, fresher tasting, easier to make and, best of all, it incorporates an element of barbecue performance theatre. For vegetarians who long to throw the tongs about, this has real possibilities. Get in there with your elbows out.

Serves 4–6 as a side dish
at a barbecue

2 spring onions (scallions),
   finely chopped
2 cloves garlic, finely chopped
3 tablespoons finely chopped
   flat-leaf parsley
juice of ½ lemon
3 tablespoons olive oil
2 eggplants (aubergines)
pinch of chilli flakes and/
   or sumac, to garnish

PITTA CRISPS
1 tablespoon olive oil
3 large round pitta breads
sea salt flakes and sumac,
   for sprinkling

TO TRANSPORT
Tuck the eggplants into a basket, along with the jar of green goodness and a fairly sturdy serving bowl, and set forth, not forgetting the chilli flakes, sumac and pitta crisps. Once you arrive at your destination, mill about a bit until your host seems to have the barbecue smoking-hot before sneaking your purple beauties onto the grill.

Place the spring onion, garlic, parsley, lemon juice, olive oil and a generous pinch of salt in a screw-top jar and mix together. Leave for an hour – or indeed overnight (in the fridge), for the flavours to mingle.

Now for the pitta crisps. Preheat the oven to 180°C (350°F). Rub a generous amount of olive oil over both sides of the pitta breads, then sprinkle with sea salt. Cut the breads into large pieces, then spread out in a single layer on a large baking sheet and bake for 8–10 minutes until golden brown. Remove from the oven, sprinkle lightly with sumac and leave to cool completely. Keep in an airtight container.

To prepare the eggplants, peel off the little sticker, if there is one, and give them a wash. That's all. Get the barbecue smoking-hot, then put the whole eggplants on the grill and close the lid, if there is one. Your work is mostly done; now it is time to mingle. Take a beer in your non-dominant hand and some heavy barbecue tongs in the other. Next, hold forth loudly and authoritatively on the batting order for the next Test/the unfeasibility of local real estate prices/recent taxi journeys you have taken.

After about 10 minutes, poke your eggplants with the tongs. If the skin is charred and flaky and the whole show looks like it is about to collapse, they are ready. Remove from the heat and leave to cool until you can *just* about handle them. Scrape off any really burnt parts that you think might be unpalatable, but keep in mind that it is not only acceptable, but absolutely advisable, to have some flecks of charred skin in the mix. Cut the eggplants in half and place in a serving bowl. Pour over the contents of your jar, then use a knife and fork to briskly and randomly cut through the eggplant, roughly chopping it into large pieces. The heat of the cooked eggplant will lightly cook the garlic, so it is important to bring the two elements together as quickly as possible.

Sprinkle with a pinch of chilli flakes or sumac before serving with pitta crisps.

Travelling cheese soufflé

Soufflé. Even though not especially tricky to make, it's a dish that retains an authentic tang of terror. And the dying-swan act of your average soufflé once it's taken out of the oven (you really need to pace out your oven-to-table route in advance, to make sure your guests get to appreciate it at peak-puffiness) is such that no-one would ever be stupid enough to try and transport one anywhere, surely. *However*. What if you did your transporting before baking? Turns out that if you sneakily add a little egg-white powder (you can get this stuff in top-shelf cooking shops), it is possible to stabilise the mixture to the point where you can spoon it into individual soufflé dishes, chill them, then tenderly carry them with you for baking on-site. My fervent thanks are due to Colleen Heikkinen of Chef and the Cook in Camperdown, Sydney, who not only planted the seed of this idea, but also dispensed useful advice and sold me the enamel cups for the prototype travelling soufflé. If your soufflé is a homebody, don't worry about the egg-white powder.

Serves 4

80 g (2¾ oz) butter, plus extra for greasing
80 g (2¾ oz) finely grated pecorino, plus extra for lining the dishes or cups
300 ml (10½ fl oz) milk
1 brown onion, halved crossways
1 fresh bay leaf
40 g (1½ oz) plain (all-purpose) flour
1 teaspoon dijon mustard
4 eggs, separated
1 teaspoon finely chopped thyme leaves
80 g (2¾ oz) grated gruyère
1 teaspoon egg-white powder
green salad, to serve

First, prepare your soufflé dishes. I used four 250 ml (9 fl oz/1 cup) enamelled tin cups, because I like the way they look, but you could use traditional ceramic soufflé ramekins, or those beautiful miniature copper pans that cost as much as a small family car but are undeniably attractive. What is most important is that you prepare them wisely, brushing the insides with vertical strokes of a butter-soaked pastry brush and then sprinkling generously with finely grated pecorino. As well as preventing stickage, this will give your soufflés a tasty crust.

In a small saucepan, heat the milk gently with the onion and the bay leaf, then let it simmer for 5 minutes to infuse the flavours. Meanwhile, melt the butter in a heavy-based saucepan over low–medium heat and add the flour, stirring and poking for about 2 minutes until the roux is cooked. Now take the onion and bay leaf out of the milk, and slowly add it to the roux, stirring all the while – it should thicken up nicely. Remove from the heat, then stir in the mustard, egg yolks, thyme, the pecorino and gruyère. Season to taste with salt and white pepper, then leave to cool to room temperature.

Recipe continued overleaf . . .

Meanwhile, whisk the egg whites with a pinch of salt to the soft-peak stage. Add the egg-white powder and whisk again. Take a third of the whisked egg whites and gently fold through the cheese mixture to loosen it. Now fold the rest of the egg whites through until nicely combined. Spoon or scrape the mixture evenly into your prepared dishes, filling them to the brim. Level off the top and stick them in the fridge.

When you want to bake the soufflés, preheat the oven to 180°C (350°F). Tie a generous collar of baking paper (for best results, grease it first – a certain amount of overkill is quite advisable here) around the dishes: aim for at least 8 cm (3¼ in) taller above the top of the dish, to allow for best-case-scenario expansion. Place the soufflés on a baking tray and bake for 15 minutes or until well risen and deep-golden, with an aroma you can no longer resist. Serve immediately with a green salad and a smug expression.

TO TRANSPORT

A word of warning: do not attempt this transfer unless you have decent suspension; the whole palaver will go badly wrong if you are getting to your destination by means of pogo stick or speed-hump-infested roads. Gentleness and stability are key here – think transplant-ready-organ gentle. When you are ready to leave, prepare a small Esky (cool box) with maximum soufflé-comfort in mind. I'm thinking rolled-up tea towels to wedge them in firmly, with ice-packs in between. Take a supply of baking paper and string with you. When you reach your destination, consign your soufflés to the fridge until the time comes to bake them.

Beetroot tarte tatin with goat's cheese and lemon thyme

Australians travelling abroad for the first time are often surprised to discover that not everyone loves beetroot as much as they do – unless, of course, they are travelling to New Zealand or the borscht-loving nations. But here is something to convert the beet-fearing. Using a sheet of ready-made puff pastry, this couldn't be easier, though I do like to roll out the pastry more thinly so the tart base doesn't end up stodgy. Or, if you want to make your own puff pastry, then hats off to you!

Serves 4

1 teaspoon butter
2 small cooked beetroot,
    cut into 1 cm (½ in) slices
50 g (1¾ oz/½ cup) grated
    cheddar cheese
1 sheet ready-rolled puff pastry
100 g (3½ oz) goat's cheese
handful of toasted walnuts
handful of rocket (arugula)

LEMON THYME
DRESSING
1 tablespoon chopped lemon
    thyme leaves
2 tablespoons olive oil
juice and finely grated zest
    of 1 lemon

TO TRANSPORT
Carry the tart in a cake tin, taking care to keep it level. Keep the rocket, cheese and walnuts aside until ready to serve, and spoon over the dressing at the last minute.

Preheat the oven to 180°C (350°F). Line the base of a 20 cm (8 in) round springform tin or loose-based tin. Put the butter into the tin and place it in the oven as it's heating up for a minute or so, just until it melts. Swirl the melted butter around to cover the base of the tin, rubbing a bit up the sides to grease them too.

Arrange the beetroot slices in the base of the tin, leaving about 1 cm (½ in) clear all around the edges – this allows the pastry to puff up, unfettered, making for a much tidier tart. Sprinkle over the cheddar, which will act like a glue between the beets and pastry.

Now carefully sit the tin on the sheet of pastry and trace around it, scoring into the pastry to give you a circle the same size as the tin. Lay the pastry on top of the beetroot, tucking in the edges just as if you were tucking the beetroot into bed. Bake for about 20 minutes or until the pastry is golden.

Meanwhile, combine the ingredients for the dressing and put aside.

When the tart is cooked, leave it to cool for a moment, then run a knife around the edge to loosen the pastry from the tin. Carefully liberate the tart from the tin, either by pushing up the loose base of the tin, or releasing the clip on the springform. Now put a serving plate face-down over the pastry and turn the whole lot upside down so your tart is now sitting on the serving plate, beetroot-side up. Gently, gently lift off the base of the tin and the baking paper. The aim is to keep the beetroot in place on the pastry, but if any does come loose, just put it back where it belongs and no-one will be any the wiser.

Serve the tart at room temperature, crumbling the goat's cheese over the top, then scattering with walnuts and rocket. Drizzle over a generous amount of the lemon thyme dressing – in this dish, the dressing really is the magic bullet.

Onion and cheddar tart

Why is cheese and onion automatically associated with the hot blush of shame? Cheese and onion chips, for instance, or weird packet soup, or some sort of doughy mess from a chain bakery store? The truth is that cheese and onion, sensitively handled, are an immortal combination. In a tart, they're hard to beat. Just keep it simple.

Serves 4–6

olive oil, for frying
3 large brown onions,
    cut into very thin crescents
splash of white wine
3 teaspoons balsamic vinegar
1 sheet ready-rolled puff pastry
5 eggs
200 g (7 oz) crème fraîche
    or thick (double) cream,
    or a mixture of both
1 teaspoon chopped chives,
    tarragon or parsley
65 g (2½ oz/⅔ cup)
    grated cheddar
12 or so cherry tomatoes,
    cut in half

Heat a generous glug of olive oil in a large frying pan over medium heat and throw in the onion, stirring to coat with the oil, then keep at it for about 3–4 minutes. A bit of browning at the edges is fine, but if your onion is becoming shrivelled little scraps, your pan is too hot. Once it has just started to soften, turn the heat down to low and leave to caramelise for another 10 minutes, returning to stir every minute or so. Drizzle in the white wine and simmer for another 3 minutes, then turn off the heat and stir through the balsamic vinegar. Have a taste – the onion should be completely without crunch, and very flavoursome.

For the tart shell, preheat the oven to 180°C (350°F). Coax the pastry into a 23 cm (9 in) loose-based fluted tart (flan) tin, then line with a piece of crumpled baking paper and pour in some baking beads or uncooked rice or beans. Bake for 12 minutes until golden.

Meanwhile, crack the eggs into a bowl, scooping out about a teaspoon of egg white into a smaller bowl. Remove the tart shell from the oven and lift out the beads and baking paper. Paint the tart shell with the reserved egg white, then return to the oven for about 5 minutes, or until the egg coating has set and turned white. Remove from the oven and reduce the temperature to 160°C (315°F).

While the tart shell is cooling, make the filling. Whisk together the eggs, crème fraîche and herbs until just combined (I find the cheddar adds enough saltiness and flavour, but feel free to season with salt and pepper if you like). To assemble, sprinkle one third of the grated cheese over the base of the tart shell, followed by the cooled onion. Pour in about half of the egg mixture, sprinkle the rest of the cheese over, and finish with the rest of the egg mixture.

Recipe continued overleaf . . .

Lunch

Now place the halved cherry tomatoes, cut-side up, artfully around the top, being ever so careful to have them float on top rather than sink down. Not only do they look prettier this way, but it will keep the tomato juice from spoiling the texture of your savoury custard.

Bake the tart for about 20 minutes: it is imperative you don't overcook this thing – you want the middle to be wobbly, as it will continue to cook a bit more and firm up once it is out of the oven.

Wait at least 10 minutes before easing the tart out of its tin (careful, now) and sliding it onto your serving plate. This tart is best eaten warm or at room temperature.

A NOTE ON AVOIDING A SOGGY BASE

Every step of the baking method above is aimed at keeping the tart base as crisp as possible. Another trick I have learned is to cook tarts on a preheated baking sheet. So, while the oven is heating up, put a baking sheet on the oven shelf to warm, and then sit the tart on this to cook – this gives the base an extra blast of heat to crisp it up quickly, before the egg mixture has a chance to seep into it and turn it soggy. Once you have the knack, there are plenty of other filling options to show off your new-found skills: salmon and dill, ham and cheese, asparagus and gruyère, baked pumpkin and feta, mushroom and tarragon.

TO TRANSPORT

If you want to take this to a friend, or as a contribution to a picnic or a lunch buffet, gently loosen the edges of the tart away from the tin, but keep it in there until you are ready to pop it out for serving.

Soft pretzels (laugenbrezel)

Okay, before you glance down, see that this is a two-day undertaking, utter a bark of contempt and browse on . . . Stop! Don't be so hasty! I make two points in this recipe's defence. One: the day-before duties are quite light. Two, a truly traditional pretzel recipe would call for the use of lard and also vats of boiling lye solution. So, by comparison, this recipe is a total doddle. I mean, you don't even need safety goggles! Butter can be used instead of lard, household bicarbonate of soda instead of lye. And the reward of freshly baked salty pretzels for you and your kin, well – enough said.

Makes 16

2 teaspoons active dried yeast
1 tablespoon golden syrup
150 ml (5 fl oz)
   lukewarm water
500 g (1 lb 2 oz) strong
   white bread flour
2 teaspoons fine salt
150 ml (5 fl oz) milk
3 tablespoons softened butter
3 tablespoons bicarbonate of
   soda (baking soda)
coarse salt and/or sesame
   seeds, to decorate

The day before, all you need to do is allocate about half an hour to make the dough. Mix the yeast and golden syrup with the water in a jug and leave to stand for about 5–10 minutes to activate the yeast.

Meanwhile, stir the flour and salt together in a large mixing bowl and make a well in the middle. Pour in the yeast mixture, along with the milk. Now gradually incorporate the flour from around the edges until a dough forms. Mix in the butter, cover and leave the dough to rest for 10 minutes.

Now, give the dough a good knead. You can do this by hand on a lightly floured bench. Or, if you want to minimise mess, leave the dough in its bowl and, using a silicone dough scraper or spatula, fold over the dough and press down to stretch it out. Give the bowl a quarter-turn and repeat. Either way, keep going for about 10 minutes until the dough is smooth and elastic. Cover the bowl with plastic wrap and refrigerate overnight.

Next day, scrape the dough out onto an un-floured surface and divide into 4 equal portions (you can weigh them if you have perfection issues), then cut each portion into 4 again, to give you 16 little pieces of dough. Roll each one into a ball. Place on a lightly floured surface and lightly flour the tops too, then cover with a clean tea towel and allow to rest for 10 minutes.

Now coax each ball into a long sausage shape, about 30 cm (12 in) long, and slightly plumper in the middle than it is at the ends. Take the two ends, lift them up and cross them over. Cross them a second time to form a little twist, then lay the ends back down, pressing them into the loop. Lightly flour the tops, cover with a clean tea towel and allow to rest for 45 minutes.

Recipe continued overleaf . . .

Preheat the oven to 200°C (400°F) and line two large baking trays.

Now comes the science experiment. Combine 1 litre (35 fl oz/4 cups) of water with the bicarbonate of soda in a large, wide pan and bring to the boil. Give each pretzel a 30-second bath in the boiling solution, then remove with a slotted spoon and place on the prepared baking trays. (This might seem like a bit of a palaver, but what you are doing is raising the pH of the pretzel surface. Not only does this hasten their browning to give them their distinctive colour, but also the residual bicarb gives the pretzels that unmistakable, quite addictive taste.)

Sprinkle the pretzels with coarse salt or sesame seeds, or both. Bake for 15–20 minutes, until the outsides are mahogany-brown, then transfer to a wire rack to cool. They will look darker than you expect because of their bicarb bath.

Eat plain, or with lots of good, cold unsalted butter.

TO TRANSPORT
Pack and go! Don't delay, as these are best eaten within half a day of baking.

Portable pizza

It's weird. Pizza is something most of us would happily pay a total stranger to deliver to our door. And yet, how often do you take one round to a mate's place? Rarely-to-never would be my guess. The advantage you have over the average pizza delivery, though, is that you can come and assemble the thing in the kitchen of the recipient. This allows for much fresher toppings; colourful, zesty stuff that would die a horrible death if consigned to a vinyl wallet on the back of a motorbike for any length of time. Just do the messy, floury stuff at home, and par-bake your bases, then pile them up with fresh toppings at your destination. Try a combination of rocket and smoked salmon or a reinvented margherita with a fennel-scented dressing. The latter is inspired by a salad from Yotam Ottolenghi, to whom Wendy and I maintain small household shrines. I am convinced he would not mind.

Makes 4 pizza bases

375 ml (13 fl oz/1½ cups)
   lukewarm water
2 teaspoons active dried yeast
2 teaspoons raw sugar
2 tablespoons olive oil, plus
   extra for drizzling and frying
500 g (1 lb 2 oz/3⅓ cups)
   strong white bread flour
½ teaspoon fine salt
sea salt and tomato passata –
   optional

Put the water in a jug, mix in the yeast, sugar and olive oil and leave to stand for 5–10 minutes to activate the yeast – when it is ready, it should be frothy and bubbling.

Mix the flour and salt in a large bowl, then form a well in the middle and pour in the yeast mixture. With a rubber spatula, slowly bring in the flour, mixing to form a dough. Cover and leave to rest for 10 minutes. Give the dough a light knead until it forms a nice smooth ball, then drizzle over some olive oil to coat it thinly. Cover the bowl and leave in a warm-ish spot for at least a couple of hours until doubled in size.

Meanwhile, get to work on your toppings (see overleaf).

When you're ready to cook the bases, preheat the oven to 240°C (475°F).

Taking a quarter of the dough at a time, stretch it out into a rough circle. If you like, you can lightly sprinkle your pizza base with sea salt (for the tomato and mozzarella topping) or spread it with a very thin layer of tomato passata (for the smoked salmon version).

Bake the pizza bases for 8–10 minutes or until slightly risen and crisp.

Recipes continued overleaf . . .

Tomato and mozzarella

Makes enough for 2 pizzas

1 teaspoon fennel seeds
1 clove garlic, roughly chopped
finely grated zest of 1 lemon
1 tablespoon chopped basil
2 tablespoons extra virgin
  olive oil, plus a little more
  for drizzling
3 ripe tomatoes, thickly sliced
12 cherry tomatoes, cut in half
300 g (10½ oz) fresh
  mozzarella, ideally buffalo
handful of basil leaves

Toast the fennel seeds in a dry frying pan over low–medium heat until aromatic, then tip into a mortar and grind to a coarse powder with a pestle. Add the garlic and lemon zest and pound into a paste. Stir in the basil and olive oil.

Divide the tomato slices between the pizza bases, tear the mozzarella over the top and spoon over the dressing. Scatter with basil leaves and drizzle with a little more olive oil.

Smoked salmon and rocket

Makes enough for 2 pizzas

150 g (5½ oz) smoked salmon
½ preserved lemon, rind only,
  finely chopped
2 tablespoons crème fraîche
  or sour cream
handful of rocket (arugula)
½ lemon, cut into wedges

Distribute twirls of smoked salmon over each pizza base, then sprinkle with preserved lemon and little dots of crème fraîche or sour cream. Scatter the rocket leaves over the top. Serve with lemon wedges for squeezing.

TO TRANSPORT
Take the cooled pizza bases swaddled in plastic wrap. No, it's not attractive, but it will stop them drying out. Carry the tomatoes, mozzarella, basil and dressing separately. For the salmon, either take all the elements and assemble on site – or, for less faffing at your destination, set everything out on a shallow tray or plate and cover with plastic wrap, then carefully lift out and arrange when the time comes. Give the bases about 3 minutes in a 120°C (235°F) oven, then pile on the room-temperature toppings and serve.

Caponata

This cross between a relish, a salad, a sauce and a stew hails from Sicily. Every day, in pocket-sized Palermo kitchens, caponata is made by laboriously frying each ingredient individually. An unnecessary complication? Well no, millions of Sicilians are not wrong. Caponata really is better if you give each component its own time in the frying pan, and the best thing about it is that it ages well. Day two is superior to day one, and it's good for up to a week.

Serves 4–6 (makes 1 x 1 litre/
35 fl oz/4 cup jar)

plenty of olive oil, for frying
3 stalks celery, finely diced
1 large red or yellow capsicum
　(pepper), diced
1 zucchini (courgette),
　finely diced
1 small eggplant (aubergine),
　finely diced
5 large tomatoes
3 cloves garlic, finely chopped
1 teaspoon grated ginger
10 large green olives, pitted
　and finely chopped
2 teaspoons capers, chopped
　– optional (they are a love/
　hate thing!)
2 teaspoons red wine vinegar
20 g (¾ oz) pine nuts
12 mint leaves, finely chopped

TO TRANSPORT
If you have a spring-lidded preserving jar, now is the time to dig it out. Caponata can be spread over toast or crackers; stirred through pasta or couscous; or served with meat or fish. Or eaten with a spoon straight from the jar. Just the thing for brand-new parents and their out-of-whack eating patterns.

The key to this recipe is gentle heat. Resist the temptation to speed things up with a brisk flame; keep your frying pan over medium heat and take care to avoid browning any of your ingredients. Finally, you should know that this dish takes a lot of olive oil – that's why it tastes nice. Give in to it.

Add a generous glug of oil to a large frying pan and fry the celery over low heat until it is starting to become translucent, then transfer to a large baking tray. Now add a glug more oil and fry the capsicum until it starts to soften, then place next to the celery on the baking tray. Repeat the process with the zucchini, and then the eggplant, adding more oil as needed.

Meanwhile, cut each tomato in half and remove the hard core area from around the stem. Grate the tomatoes on a large box grater into a bowl, discarding the skins. Watch your knuckles!

Wipe out the frying pan. Fry the chopped garlic for a few seconds in a little more oil, then rescue it from burning by stirring in about a quarter of the grated tomato. Cook for a minute or two until the sauce has reduced slightly and the aroma of garlic is filling your kitchen. Add the rest of the tomato and cook for another 2 minutes until the sauce is reduced. Sneak in the grated ginger at the last minute. Yes, I know putting ginger into a traditional caponata might cause a thousand nonnas to take to the streets and burn this book, if only they knew about it – but in my opinion it is a pleasant and not unreasonable addition. Now pour the tomato sauce over your vegetables on the baking tray, stir everything together and tuck away in a 140°C (275°F) oven for 25 minutes.

Leave to cool, then scatter over the olives, capers (if using), red wine vinegar, pine nuts and mint. If not serving straightaway, transfer to a clean jar and pour in enough olive oil to cover the surface. Refrigerate for up to a week.

Mushroom and sherry empanadas

Empanadas, those versatile little pasties found all over South America, can quite respectably be either baked or fried. But after extensive experimentation, I've come to the confronting realisation that – despite the calorific penalty – fried is truly the way to go. Anything else, as Paul Keating might have said, is camping out. Only when you fry them do you get the deep golden colour, the happy little crispy pastry bubbles, and that general 'doughnuts at the fair' feeling. The sherry in the pastry mix gives an extra depth and sweetness, and the chipotle gives the filling a nice smoky kick.

Makes 16

1 small red onion, diced
1 clove garlic, finely chopped
olive oil, for frying
200 g (7 oz) mushrooms, diced
1 ear sweetcorn, kernels sliced
    off the cob
1 chipotle chilli in adobo
3 teaspoons sherry vinegar
150 g (5½ oz) mozzarella,
    fontina or provolone, cut
    into 1 cm (½ in) cubes
large handful of coriander
    (cilantro) leaves, chopped
vegetable oil, for deep-frying

SHERRY PASTRY

300 g (10½ oz/2 cups) plain
    (all-purpose) flour
1 teaspoon baking powder
80 ml (2½ fl oz/⅓ cup)
    olive oil
2½ tablespoons dry sherry
2½ tablespoons iced water
1 teaspoon fine salt

TO TRANSPORT

These pack well for a picnic or a jaunt to a friend's place. To reheat, give them a quick blast in a 180°C (350°F) oven until warmed through.

For the pastry, mix all the ingredients in a bowl until the mixture clumps together. Hand mix and then knead for several minutes to make a smooth dough; add more flour if the dough is sticky and adheres to the table, or more water if it's floury. Wrap in plastic wrap and chill for 30 minutes.

Meanwhile, make the filling: fry the onion and garlic in a glug of olive oil until soft and starting to caramelise, about 15 minutes. Add a little more oil, along with the mushroom, and cook until it is soft and beginning to brown. Add the corn kernels and the chipotle chilli and cook for a minute, then remove from the heat and stir through the sherry vinegar.

Cut the chilled pastry in half, and keep cutting in half again, until you have 16 blobs of pastry. Roll out into thin rounds about 12 cm (4½ in) across. Put a tablespoon of the mushroom mixture, 2 cubes of cheese and some coriander in the middle, then fold the pastry over to make a little pasty. Press the edges together firmly. This is your opportunity to create a swanky empanada with pleated edging. Fold one corner of the pastry in, then keep folding and pinching until the edge is rolled and tightly sealed. There are umpteen online videos that are more helpful than my written description could ever be; just search for 'empanadas' and *'repulgue'*, which is the fabulous Spanish term for this exact pleating process.

Seriously, though – let's not lose focus. *WE ARE HERE FOR THE FRYING.* If you can't be bothered with the *repulgue*, just seal the edges with the tines of a fork, which will give you a nice crimped effect.

Frying time: heat at least a 5 cm (2 in) depth of oil in a heavy-based saucepan, or use a deep fryer. Heat to 180°C (350°F), or to the point where a cube of bread browns nicely in 15 seconds. Cook the empanadas in batches, turning them so they brown evenly. Drain well on paper towel.

Smoked mozzarella tart

I first came across smoked mozzarella in Seville, in a tiny bar where they bunged a couple of thick slices into an earthenware dish, grilled it until smoky and bubbling, then served it with crackers. The sheer effrontery of the dish (just cheese!) was pleasing enough, but the cheese itself – delicious. Sometimes billed as *scamorza affumicata*, it's available in Italian delis; in this tart, it adds a smoky flavour that works nicely with the sticky sweet potato, caramelised red onion and salty olives. I've included a pastry recipe, but if you're in a rush there's no disgrace in using bought. Serve with a big green salad, or a tangle of rocket dressed with half olive oil and half pomegranate molasses.

Serves 8

2 tablespoons olive oil
1 tablespoon
  pomegranate molasses
1 large sweet potato (about
  600 g/1 lb 5 oz), cut into
  2.5 cm (1 in) cubes
2 red onions, cut into wedges
20 fat kalamata olives, pitted
2 eggs
300 ml (10½ fl oz) sour cream
50 g (1¾ oz) parmesan, grated
125 g (4½ oz) smoked
  mozzarella, cut into
  1 cm (½ in) cubes
6 thyme sprigs
2 tablespoons pine nuts
SHORTCRUST PASTRY
300 g (10½ oz/2 cups) plain
  (all purpose) flour
125 g (4½ oz) chilled
  butter, cubed
1 egg yolk
iced water

TO TRANSPORT
Carry in a basket under a tea towel. Either serve at room temperature, or reheat for about 10 minutes in a 160°C (315°F) oven.

For the pastry, pulse the flour and butter in a food processor to coarse crumbs. Plop in your egg yolk and pulse until it starts to clump together. Add icy-cold water, teaspoon by teaspoon, until you have a big lump of dough. Remove and press into a disc with your hands, then wrap in plastic wrap and chill for at least 30 minutes.

Preheat the oven to 180°C (350°F) and grease a tart tin; I used a 30 x 10 cm (12 x 4 in) fluted oblong tin, but you could use a round one of about 25 cm (10 in) diameter, or several smaller tins to make individual tarts for a picnic.

Place your chilled pastry between two sheets of baking paper and roll out to a thickness of about 3 mm (⅛ in). Lay the pastry carefully into the tin, pressing and pleating it so it fits smoothly; trim the edges. Chill the tart shell for 10 minutes, then line with a piece of crumpled baking paper and pour in some baking beads or uncooked rice or beans. Bake for 10 minutes until golden. Remove the paper and baking beads, then set aside to cool.

Jack up the oven to 200°C (400°F). In a large bowl, whisk together the olive oil and pomegranate molasses, then toss the sweet potato and onion through until they're coated and glistening. Tip into a baking tray and roast until caramelised and soft, about 30 minutes; add the olives for the last 5 minutes. Reduce the oven temperature to 180°C (350°F).

In a jug, whisk together the eggs, sour cream and parmesan, seasoning to taste with salt and pepper. Pack the tart shell tightly with the sweet potato, onion and olives, then poke the mozzarella into any gaps you can find. Pour the egg mixture evenly over the top. Sprinkle the thyme sprigs and pine nuts artfully around the place, then bake for 30 minutes, or until the tart is puffy and golden.

Dinner

Papillotes

If I had to nominate one piece of kitchen kit I couldn't live without (and you'd be surprised how much idle thought one person can devote to this exact question), I think it might actually be baking paper. It's great for prepping and lining, for rolling out and freezing, and when employed as tracing paper, it can keep small children occupied for sufficient time to let you make a cake. But the art of cooking food *en papillote* surely signals baking paper's finest hour. It's dramatic, it allows food to cook in its own vapours, and it renders individual portions neatly portable. If there is going to be a delay between wrapping and cooking, a foil liner added to the base of your papillotes before filling is a wise precaution. And the parcels need to be carried on a baking tray, but a few of those flat ice-packs wrapped in a tea towel would cover you for short journeys. Otherwise, think of an Esky (cool box).

For your convenience, here are three suggestions for dishes *en papillote*. First up, a Vietnamese-style concoction that cunningly circumvents the single weakness of *en papillote* cookery (a tendency for greens to go dark and limp) by piling in fresh herbs post-baking. Next, Greek-style baked fish, and finally, mixed mushrooms luxuriating in a velvety umami bath of miso butter; trust me, once you've tasted miso butter, you'll probably think about drinking it straight. Or maybe that's just me.

Vietnamese-style fish salad

Serves 4

2 carrots, cut into matchsticks
4 x 150 g (5½ oz) fillets of
  white fish, skin removed
1 lime, very thinly sliced
100 g (3½ oz) snow peas
  (mangetout), finely shredded
handful each of coriander
  (cilantro), mint and basil
  leaves, torn
50 g (1¾ oz/⅓ cup)
  roasted cashews
1 small chilli, thinly sliced

DRESSING
2 tablespoons brown sugar
2 tablespoons caster
  (superfine) sugar
2 tablespoons fish sauce
2 tablespoons lime juice

First make the dressing. Put the sugars in a small non-reactive saucepan with 2 tablespoons of water and bring to the boil. Let the caramel bubble away until it turns a toffee colour, then allow to cool slightly before adding the fish sauce and lime juice.

Take 4 sheets of baking paper and fold each one in half, so you end up with something a bit smaller than A4, then cut out a half-loveheart shape and open it out. Time to fill your parcels: pile up a little raft of the carrots, set the fish on top, then finish with a couple of slices of lime. Start at the pointy end of the heart and fold narrow pleats along the edge until you have reached the top end of the heart. Give each end a twist to seal securely. Toss the snowpeas with the herbs, cashews and chilli.

When you are almost ready to eat, preheat the oven to 200°C (400°F). Place your parcels on a baking tray and cook for 8–10 minutes until the fish is just cooked. To serve, carefully open the parcels and add a tangle of the snowpea and herb mixture, then spoon over the dressing.

Greek-style fish with fennel and green olives

Serves 4

3 large tomatoes, cut in half
olive oil, for frying
3 cloves garlic, finely chopped
pinch of fennel seeds or
   coriander seeds
60 ml (2 fl oz/¼ cup) dry
   white wine
150 g (5 oz) large green
   olives, pitted
20 g (¾ oz) flat-leaf parsley,
   leaves only
1½ tablespoons lemon juice
1 large or 2 small fennel bulbs,
   cut lengthways into 1 cm
   (½ in) slices
4 x 150 g (5½ oz) fillets of
   white fish or salmon
couscous and toasted pine
   nuts, to serve

First get to work on the tomato halves with a box grater perched over a bowl to catch the juices, grating the flesh until you get to the skin; discard the skins.

Heat a generous glug of olive oil in a heavy-based frying pan over low heat. Add the garlic, along with the fennel or coriander seeds – and, after only about 15 seconds, add the tomato pulp with all its juices. We want to avoid, at all costs, the garlic turning brown. Let the sauce reduce down a bit by letting it bubble away gently for a few minutes, stirring occasionally. Add a splash of dry white wine and repeat the simmering/ reducing process for another few minutes. For this purpose, the sauce should still be quite thin and runny. Season with a pinch of salt.

Chop the olives together with the parsley until you have a very chunky pesto. Transfer to a bowl and stir through all but 2 teaspoons of the lemon juice, adding salt to taste.

Take 4 sheets of baking paper and fold each one in half, so you end up with something a bit smaller than A4, then cut out a half-loveheart shape and open it out. Time to fill your parcels: start with a layer of fennel slices, then the fish (skin removed, if it is salmon), followed by a generous amount of the tomato sauce. Finish with a squeeze of lemon – and, if you like, another tiny dash of wine – then start at the pointy end of the heart and fold narrow pleats along the edge until you have reached the top end of the heart. Give each end a twist to seal securely.

When you are almost ready to eat, preheat the oven to 220°C (425°F). Place your parcels on a baking tray and cook for about 10 minutes. Remove from the oven and leave to rest, unopened, for another 5 minutes. Adjust the cooking time down slightly if you are using a delicate white fish, or increase it a little if you have a particularly chunky piece of salmon.

Lift the parcels onto individual plates, and let your guests (carefully) open their parcel and help themselves to a generous spoonful of olive and parsley pesto. Serve with couscous and toasted pine nuts.

Recipes continued overleaf...

Mushrooms with miso butter

Serves 4

2 zucchini (courgettes)
500 g (1 lb 2 oz)
   mixed mushrooms
1 tablespoon tamari, or other
   light soy sauce
2 tablespoons lime juice
rice or couscous and coriander
   (cilantro) leaves, to serve

MISO BUTTER
125 g (4½ oz) butter
1 clove garlic, finely chopped
2 thin spring onions
   (scallions), finely chopped
60 g (2¼ oz) white miso paste
1 teaspoon lime juice
1 tablespoon finely chopped
   flat-leaf parsley

A NOTE ON
MISO BUTTER
As a pre-sliced roll of miso
butter is such a handy thing
to have in the freezer, this
recipe makes more than you
need – you'll thank me for
it as you melt a slice over
steamed vegetables, baked
potatoes, salmon or steak
for instant flavour pizzazz.

First, make the miso butter. Roughly dice 80 g (2¾ oz) of the butter, put it in a bowl and leave somewhere warm to soften. Melt the remaining butter in a small saucepan over gentle heat, then stir in the garlic. Leave it on the heat until it just starts to bubble, then take off the heat and stir in the spring onion. Set aside to cool slightly. Stir the miso paste into the bowl of softened butter, then pour in the melted butter mixture and use a wooden spoon to give it a really thorough mix. Finally, stir through the lime juice, parsley and a couple of grindings of pepper. Scrape the butter onto a piece of plastic wrap, patting it into a long sausage shape. Roll up tightly and refrigerate until needed; the miso butter will keep well for up to 2 weeks in the fridge (or for several months in the freezer).

Use a vegetable peeler or small sharp knife to shave the zucchini into ribbons. Thickly slice half the mushrooms and put in a bowl, then sprinkle over the tamari and lime juice. The mushrooms will suck up the liquid almost as quickly as you can put it in there, so stir through quickly before leaving the mushrooms to absorb the flavours for just a minute or two.

When you are almost ready to eat, preheat the oven to 220°C (425°F). Take 4 sheets of baking paper and fold each one in half, so you end up with something a bit smaller than A4, then cut out a half-loveheart shape and open it out. Time to fill your parcels: place a quarter of the zucchini ribbons on each sheet of baking paper, followed by a quarter of the mushrooms and a couple of slices of miso butter (about a tablespoon per parcel). Start at the pointy end of the heart and fold narrow pleats along the edge until you have reached the top end of the heart. Give each end a twist to seal securely. Place your parcels on a baking tray and cook for about 8 minutes or until the vegetables are just done.

This is lovely served with brown or white rice and some coriander, but if you're in a hurry, couscous will do nicely.

Spaghetti lentilaise

If a family has a signature recipe, then this is Wendy's. She pioneered lentilaise in some dark, sleep-deprived moment of immortal brilliance, and it now turns up on the dinner table every week. It remains popular to the extent that it is requested for birthday meals. It is carb-comfort with exactly the right degree of saltiness, sweetness and tomatoey-ness – and of course it must be finished royally with cheese (and perhaps a shake of chilli or Worcestershire sauce for the adults). If you feel that your children/other half/innocent recipient-to-be of a food parcel would not come at lentils, I urge you to suspend your scepticism and give it a try. You could use 100 g (3½ oz/ ½ cup) of dried Puy-style lentils instead of the tinned – just add an extra tomato tin's worth of water and extend the cooking time by 20 minutes.

Serves 4–6

olive oil, for frying
   and drizzling
1 large onion, finely chopped
2 stalks celery, finely diced
2 carrots, finely diced
150 g (5½ oz) button or
   chestnut mushrooms,
   finely chopped
2 tablespoons tomato paste
   (concentrated purée)
splash of red or white wine
1 x 400 g (14 oz) tin tomatoes
1 x 400 g (14 oz) tin brown
   or green lentils, rinsed
   and drained
1 teaspoon dried Italian herbs
3 large cloves garlic,
   finely chopped
1½ tablespoons finely chopped
   flat-leaf parsley – or more,
   to taste
cooked spaghetti or penne
   and finely grated parmesan,
   to serve

Place a large, lidded frying pan over medium heat and add a generous glug of olive oil. Throw in the onion and fry gently for 2–3 minutes, then add the celery and carrot and fry for 2 minutes. Toss in the mushrooms and fry for another minute. Take care not to let anything burn – turn down the heat if necessary. Stir in the tomato paste and cook for another minute.

Now donate a splash of whatever you are drinking – I prefer red – to the pan and let it sizzle for a minute or so. Next, add the tomatoes, then fill the tin half full of water (or lentil stock, if you happen to have any on hand from making the salad on page 51), swish it around and add that to the pan too. Finally stir in the lentils and the dried herbs, then adjust the heat to barely simmering, cover with the lid and leave to cook for around 15 minutes until the vegetables are tender and the sauce is thick.

Remove from the heat and stir through the garlic and parsley. The garlic adds a fresh flavour, but the residual heat will take off its sharp edge. (If you are on a mission to inject more greens into your meals, you can double or triple the amount of parsley – just make sure it is very finely chopped, and simmer it for a few minutes in the sauce.)

Drizzle with another glug of olive oil, then serve with spaghetti or penne and lots and lots of parmesan.

TO TRANSPORT
Lentilaise travels nicely and is delicious reheated. As you might imagine, the sauce is perfect freezer fodder, so while it might not be pretty, a takeaway container full of lentilaise would be suitable to drop off to any time-strapped household. Send a tub of parmesan and the dried pasta separately.

Vegetarian 'cassoulet'

A traditional cassoulet, from the Languedoc region of southern France, usually involves heavy casualties from the animal kingdom; there'll be several different porky bits, plus goose fat, duck confit and sometimes mutton. This one uses mushrooms and fennel, and leaves the barnyard undisturbed, but keeps the white beans, herbs and the nice crusty topping.

Serves 6–8

1 large onion, chopped
olive oil, for frying
2 carrots, diced
2 stalks celery, diced
1 small fennel bulb, diced
2 tablespoons tomato paste
  (concentrated purée)
3 cloves garlic, finely chopped
150 g (5½ oz)
  mushrooms, sliced
250 ml (9 fl oz/1 cup) light
  vegetable stock or water
250 ml (9 fl oz/1 cup) dry
  white wine
1 x 400 g (14 oz) tin white
  beans, rinsed and drained
2 small tomatoes, chopped
3 tablespoons chopped
  flat-leaf parsley
1 teaspoon thyme leaves

SCONE TOPPING
200 g (7 oz/1⅓ cups) plain
  (all-purpose) flour
90 g (3¼ oz) fine
  polenta (cornmeal)
1 tablespoon baking powder
1 teaspoon dried thyme
30 g (1 oz/¼ cup)
  chopped walnuts
60 g (2¼ oz) grated cheese
1 egg
25 g (1 oz) butter, melted
170 ml (5½ fl oz/⅔ cup) milk
2 tablespoons vegetable oil

If you have a big cast-iron casserole, haul it out so you can cook and bake this all in one pot. If not, never mind; just make up the vegetable part in a large frying pan and transfer it to an ovenproof dish for the baking.

In your casserole or frying pan, fry the onion in a generous amount of olive oil over medium heat for 3 minutes, stirring. Add the carrots, celery and fennel to the pan and cook for another 3 minutes, stirring so the vegetables don't stick – add more oil if necessary. Give the tomato paste and garlic a minute or two in the pan, stirring attentively so they don't catch and burn, then add the mushrooms and cook for another minute. Pour in the stock or water and wine, followed by the beans, tomato, parsley and thyme. Stir to combine and leave to simmer while you make the topping.

In a large bowl, mix together the flour, polenta, baking powder, dried thyme, walnuts and cheese. Make a well in the centre, crack your egg into it and start to combine, then add the butter, milk and oil and mix until the dough just comes together – it will be a bit sticky.

Preheat the oven to 180°C (350°F). If you were using a frying pan for your vegetables, transfer them to a deep ovenproof dish. The scone topping will absorb quite a bit of liquid, so make sure your stew is quite runny – splash in a little more water or wine if needed. Drop tablespoonfuls of the dough directly onto the hot vegetables, placing them around the edge, as if you were filling in the numbers on an imaginary clock face. Make a smaller ring inside the outer one and keep going until the vegetables are mostly covered with balls of dough. Immediately bake your cassoulet for about 25 minutes or until the scone topping is crisp and golden.

TO TRANSPORT
Wait until the cassoulet has cooled completely before covering with a lid or some foil. Drop off at its destination with instructions to reheat in a preheated 160°C (315°F) oven, covered, for 5 minutes, and then uncovered for another 5 minutes.

Moroccan chickpea and halloumi bake

This is the best kind of fast food, and employs the 'why-didn't-we-think-of-this-earlier' innovation of a halloumi crust. Even carnivores like this . . . especially if it's served with roast lamb!

Serves 6

1 red onion, coarsely chopped
olive oil, for frying
½ teaspoon ground cumin
½ teaspoon ground cinnamon
¼ teaspoon ground coriander
¼ teaspoon ground allspice
pinch of hot paprika or
    chilli powder
1 x 400 g (14 oz) tin chickpeas
250 g (9 oz) cherry tomatoes
100 g (3½ oz) spinach leaves,
    thoroughly washed
2 tablespoons chopped
    flat-leaf parsley
250 g (9 oz) halloumi,
    cut into 5 mm (¼ in) slices
juice of ½ lemon
handful of coriander
    (cilantro) leaves
couscous, to serve

Preheat the oven to 180°C (350°F).

Fry up the onion with a generous glug of olive oil in a large frying pan for about 4–5 minutes, or until it starts to soften. Add the spices and fry for another 2 minutes, stirring constantly, then tip in the chickpeas, along with a few tablespoons of their liquid, and mix well. Next add the tomatoes, spinach and parsley and stir everything around until the spinach is *just* wilted. Season with a dash of pepper.

Transfer to a shallow baking dish and cover with rows of halloumi slices. Bake for about 20 minutes until the halloumi is just starting to turn golden on the edges.

Squeeze the lemon juice over the top and sprinkle with a good handful of coriander leaves. Serve with lots of couscous.

TO TRANSPORT
One of the most delicious things on this good earth is freshly fried halloumi. But one of the worst things is 5-minute-old fried halloumi – it so quickly becomes a nasty, rubbery abomination. Baking it on a bed of chickpeas partly overcomes this problem, as the lingering heat and moisture gives the halloumi a slightly longer window of gooeyness, but it is still a fickle cheese that won't reheat well at all. If you are taking this off-site, have it all assembled but wait to bake your bake until just before you're ready to eat.

Pearl barley and lentil orzotto

Risotto is not a dish best served cold. Or reheated. In fact, it's a disaster unless you go straight from pot to plate. So, how to recreate the effect of a big bowl of warming creamy grains, but avoid the tyranny of an impatient risotto?

Barley is the key. Better known as a bulker-out of soups made by grandmothers on Saturday mornings, it also stands in well for rice, but gives an extra level of bite. The inspiration for this orzotto comes from a soup made by Kiwi chef and kitchen demi-god Peter Gordon. The combination of rosemary, porcini and parmesan is so earthy – so meaty, almost – that even your hardiest beast-a-day diners will enjoy the taste, and we've taken it upon ourselves to add even more earthiness in the form of mushrooms and lentils.

Serves 4–6

1 large brown onion,
   finely chopped
1 tablespoon finely chopped
   fresh rosemary
olive oil, for frying
   and roasting
200 g (7 oz) pearl barley
splash of red or white wine
800 ml (28 fl oz)
   vegetable stock
5 g (⅛ oz) dried porcini
   mushrooms, finely chopped
50 g (1¾ oz) Puy-style
   lentils, rinsed
300 g (10½ oz) pumpkin,
   peeled and cut into 5 cm
   (2 in) cubes
butter, for frying
250 g (9 oz) button or
   chestnut mushrooms,
   quartered
1 teaspoon tamari sauce
   or lemon juice
rocket (arugula) and finely
   grated parmesan, to serve

Fry up the onion and rosemary in a glug of olive oil in a stockpot or large saucepan over medium heat until the onion starts to soften. Add the barley and stir to coat in the oil, then pour in the wine and let it sizzle for a minute or so. Now add the stock, porcini and lentils. Bring to the boil, then turn the heat down to low and simmer for about 30 minutes or until the barley and lentils are just tender.

Meanwhile, preheat the oven to 180°C (350°F) and lightly oil a baking tray. Scatter the pumpkin over the tray, drizzle with a little more oil and roast for 20 minutes or until tender.

Melt some butter in a medium frying pan over medium–high heat and toss the mushrooms around for a few minutes until cooked to your liking. Just as you take them off the heat, sprinkle with the tamari or lemon juice.

If the orzotto seems a little wet, crank up the heat for a few minutes to reduce the liquid down. Serve in wide shallow bowls, covered with pumpkin and mushrooms, and garnished with rocket and parmesan.

TO TRANSPORT
If you intend to take this to someone's house – or just to serve it later – combine the pumpkin and mushrooms and keep them separately from the orzotto. The barley and lentils should be reheated in a saucepan (with a dash of extra water if it seems gluggy), and, as long as no-one is looking, the pumpkin and mushrooms could be gently reheated in the microwave. Pack a little bag of rocket too, as well as some parmesan.

'Pantry challenge' gratin

In the weeks before my partner Jeremy and I moved back to Australia from London, we enforced the 'pantry challenge', whereby every meal had to be cooked using something in the cupboard, so we could run our pantry reserves down to nix. For no good reason I can think of, I had at some stage bought a five-kilo bag of quinoa, so that went into tuna patties and some sort of quinoa sushi, to which I'm afraid Wendy was repeatedly subjected. Anyway, there's no quinoa at all in this recipe, but it does mostly use things you might have lurking in your cupboard. Great for when friends drop in, as they say – or, more saliently, very good for whipping up and sticking in a basket for baking on-site in the home of another. This gratin is very rich, so we've sized it as a side dish. It goes well with many things; some Puy-style lentils or a crisp green salad is a good idea too.

Serves 4

1 leek, well washed and outer green leaves discarded, finely chopped

olive oil, for frying

a little white wine or water, if needed

175 g (6 oz) cooked cannellini beans

75 g (2½ oz) crème fraîche or sour cream

2½ tablespoons cream

1 tablespoon dijon mustard

1 x 335 g (11¾ oz) jar white asparagus, drained

30 g (1 oz/½ cup) coarse fresh breadcrumbs

50 g (1¾ oz/½ cup) finely grated parmesan

2 tablespoons finely chopped flat-leaf parsley

Preheat the oven to 160°C (315°F).

In a frying pan over low–medium heat, fry the leek in the smallest amount of oil, adding a little white wine or water if it starts to stick. When the leek has wilted a bit, take the pan off the heat and mix in the beans. Mix the two creams with the mustard until smooth. Take a shallow baking dish about 20 x 15 cm (8 x 6 in) and spread about a tablespoon of the cream mixture over the base. Lay the asparagus spears on top, spoon over the leek and bean mixture, then pour over the rest of the cream mixture.

Combine the breadcrumbs, parmesan and parsley, then sprinkle over the gratin. (Just by the by, I recommend having a secret stash of this gratin topping in the freezer, ready to sprinkle at a minute's notice – it is also good on lasagne and other baked pasta dishes.) Bake your gratin for about 25 minutes, or until it is crispy, with bubbling cream underneath.

TO TRANSPORT
Par-bake the gratin for about 15 minutes and leave to cool prior to transporting, then finish cooking at your destination, just before serving.

Tomato salad spaghetti

For a friend in need of some comfort food, this is a high-class pasta sauce in a jar – taking what Paul Newman started and making it so much better. Just attach a sticky note with bullet points on how to prepare, although you can probably leave out the Italian cooking lesson. Might look a little . . . controlling? While we're on the subject of 'controlling', you should forget about this dish altogether unless you are in possession of decent tomatoes, which is to say nice deep-red, fragrant ones that have not been in your fridge getting so chilly they have forgotten they are tomatoes.

Serves 4

5 large, tasty tomatoes –
   a mix of vine-ripened
   and heirloom works well
4 spring onions (scallions)
3 large cloves garlic, cut
   in half and any green
   shoot removed
10 kalamata olives – optional
2½ tablespoons olive oil,
   plus extra for drizzling
1 tablespoon chopped
   flat-leaf parsley
500 g (1 lb 2 oz)
   dried spaghetti
basil or rocket (arugula)
   leaves and finely grated
   parmesan, to serve

Coarsely chop the tomatoes and transfer to a medium bowl, being sure to take all the juices with you. Finely chop the spring onions and garlic, and cut slivers of olive (if you are using them) off the stones. Add all this to the tomatoes, along with the olive oil, parsley and a generous pinch of salt, to make a kind of tasty salad. Leave in the fridge for at least an hour, or up to a day, to let the garlic and onion flavour permeate the oil and tomatoes.

When you are almost ready to eat, put your spaghetti in a pan of rapidly boiling salted water. Place the largest frying pan you have over medium–high heat and, when it is hot, tip in your tomato salad, all at once. Stir gently for about 2 minutes. Let it bubble away to reduce the liquid slightly, but turn down the heat if anything seems to be browning.

Once the pasta is al dente, drain well and throw it straight into the frying pan with the tomatoes. Now here comes what I see as the money step. Keeping the pan over the heat, fold the sauce through the spaghetti. Then, if your wrists are strong enough, lift the pan, tossing to make the spaghetti 'jump' in the pan – in other words, *saltare la pasta in padella* – just like you see on television. If you are a weakling or lacking in kitchen confidence, use a spatula to toss the spaghetti over and over. The sauce starts to somehow melt onto the spaghetti, and this is what makes it so damn delicious. Well, that, and the unreasonable quantities of oil and salt I add.

Transfer the spaghetti to a serving plate and scatter a handsome amount of basil or rocket over. Finish with parmesan, of course.

TO TRANSPORT
Pack up the tomato salad in a preserving jar, along with a packet of dried spaghetti and a tub of freshly grated parmesan.

Roast-everything old-fashioned vegetarian lasagne

Those who seek an authentic Italian lasagne, walk away now. This one doesn't have meat, it employs a mixture of very un-Italian cheeses, and the sauce isn't slow-cooked, more like no-cooked. And you can whip it up in a jiffy, using whatever unloved veg you have skulking in the bottom of the fridge.

Serves 8–10

1 small onion, cut into wedges
3 tomatoes, cut into wedges
1 eggplant (aubergine), cut into 2 cm (½ in) cubes
1 red capsicum (pepper), cut into 2 cm (½ in) cubes
1 yellow capsicum (pepper), cut into 2 cm (½ in) cubes
2 small zucchini (courgettes), cut into 2 cm (½ in) cubes
olive oil, for drizzling
250 g (9 oz) mushrooms, quartered
1 tablespoon lemon juice
4 large cloves garlic, crushed
2 tablespoons finely chopped flat-leaf parsley
1 teaspoon dried oregano
1 x 500 ml (17 fl oz/2 cup) jar tomato passata
250 g (9 oz) pre-cooked dried lasagne sheets
250 g (9 oz) mixed cheeses – any (or all) of crumbled feta, ricotta and grated cheddar
30 g (1 oz/½ cup, lightly packed) fresh breadcrumbs
70 g (2½ oz/⅔ cup) finely grated parmesan

WHITE SAUCE
50 g (1¾ oz) butter
40 g (1½ oz) plain (all-purpose) flour
600 ml (21 fl oz) milk

Preheat the oven to 160°C (315°F). Oil two large baking trays or dishes (about 30 x 20 cm/12 x 8 in); one of these will be used to cook and serve the lasagne, so make sure it is deep enough (at least 7 cm/2¾ in). Spread the onion and tomatoes over one baking tray, then lay the eggplant, capsicums and zucchini over the other. Drizzle both trays of veg with olive oil and season with salt, then roast for 15 minutes. Toss the mushrooms in a little olive oil and lemon juice and add to the trays of veg, wherever you can find room, and roast for another 5 minutes.

While the vegetables are roasting, make the white sauce. Melt the butter in a heavy-based saucepan over low heat, then sprinkle in the flour and stir for a couple of minutes. Remove from the heat and slowly add the milk, whisking constantly until smooth. Return the pan to the heat and keep stirring until the sauce has thickened.

Transfer the roast vegetables to a large bowl (but leave the oven on, ready for the lasagne) and stir through the garlic, parsley and oregano. Now it's assembly time. Start with a layer of passata on the base of the deeper baking tray or dish (don't bother washing off the left-over oily goodness), then a layer of lasagne sheets, leaving at least a 5 mm (¼ in) gap between the dish and the edges of the pasta. Now spread over a generous layer of passata, then a third of the roast veg, followed by a third of the cheese(s). Repeat these layers three times, gently squashing down as you go, then finish with a lid of lasagne sheets. Pour any remaining passata into the gaps between the pasta and the dish, then pour over as much of the white sauce as will fit. Mix together the breadcrumbs and parmesan and sprinkle over the top. Bake for 45–60 minutes or until well browned and piping hot.

TO TRANSPORT
If you are taking this lasagne to a third party – and really, is there any more welcome sight on your doorstep than a lasagne? – reduce the baking time to about 30 minutes and leave instructions for a further 30 minutes in a 160°C (315°F) oven at the other end.

The imam's moussaka

While this contains all the elements of a vegetarian moussaka – eggplant, potato, lentils, tomato and a white sauce – its method borrows heavily from that other great eggplant concoction, the Turkish dish called *imam bayildi*, or 'fainting imam', the clergyman in question having supposedly lost consciousness due to the dish's extreme deliciousness.

Serves 6

olive oil, for brushing
  and frying
2 large potatoes, peeled
  and thinly sliced
125 g (4½ oz) feta
½ teaspoon dried oregano
125 ml (4 fl oz/¼ cup)
  milk – optional
3 eggplants (aubergines)
2 brown or white onions,
  coarsely chopped
3 cloves garlic, finely chopped
1 tablespoon tomato paste
  (concentrated purée)
1 x 400 g (14 oz) tin tomatoes
1 large tomato, finely chopped
20 g (¾ oz) flat-leaf parsley,
  finely chopped
1½ teaspoons balsamic vinegar
pinch of ground cinnamon
squeeze of lemon juice
100 g (3½ oz/½ cup) cooked
  brown or green lentils –
  from a tin is fine

YOGHURT SAUCE
200 ml (7 fl oz)
  Greek-style yoghurt
1 small clove garlic, crushed
a few gratings of lemon zest
1½ teaspoons lemon juice
handful of finely chopped
  herbs, such as dill, parsley,
  mint and coriander
  (cilantro) – any or all

For the yoghurt sauce, combine all the ingredients with a pinch of salt, then set aside for the flavours to combine while you make the rest of the dish.

Preheat the oven to 150°C (300°F) and lightly oil a baking dish. Place a layer of potato slices in the baking dish, covering the base. Crumble some feta over the top, and sprinkle with some of the dried oregano. Repeat these layers until the potato and oregano are gone, but save some of the feta to crumble over the eggplant later. Pour the milk (or just use water) over the potatoes, slide the dish into the oven and bake for 20 minutes. Cut the eggplants in half and score the cut sides in a diamond pattern. Place on a baking tray, cut-side up, and brush with olive oil. Have the eggplants join the potatoes in the oven and keep cooking for 25 minutes.

To make a tomato sauce, fry the onions in a large frying pan with a little olive oil over low heat until translucent. Add the garlic and tomato paste and stir around for a minute or so. Drain the tinned tomatoes (reserving the liquid) and add to the pan, along with the chopped tomato and parsley. Let it simmer away for about 5 minutes, then season with salt and add a glug of olive oil. Use a wooden spoon to break up the tomatoes, then remove from the heat and stir in the balsamic vinegar.

When the eggplants and potatoes are both done, pour the reserved tomato juice over the potatoes, and arrange the eggplants on top, with their cut sides facing up. Stir the cinnamon and lemon juice through the lentils, then make a small depression in the now-slightly-deflated eggplant halves and nestle your lentils in here. Spoon tomato sauce over each eggplant and crumble over the rest of the feta. Cover with foil and bake for 1 hour.

Serve warm, rather than hot, with the yoghurt sauce.

TO TRANSPORT
This is a complete, all-in-one, ready-to-drop-off kind of meal. Cover with foil and leave instructions for reheating at 140°C (275°F) for about 10 minutes. Take the yoghurt sauce separately in a little jar.

Outdoors Thai green curry

Okay, this may be radical, but Thai curry can be great for a barbecue. Instead of being poached in a spicy bath, the ingredients are seared on the barbie and then smothered in the sauce. Advantages? The beauty of grill-marks on colourful vegetables, and the smoky satisfaction of barbecued anything.

Serves 6–8

8–12 baby eggplants
   (aubergines), or 1 large one
2 red or yellow
   capsicums (peppers)
50 g (1¾ oz) flat or
   cup mushrooms
2 zucchini (courgettes)
100 g (3½ oz) baby sweetcorn
100 g (3½ oz) snow peas
   (mangetout)
6 spring onions (scallions)
150 g (5½ oz) asparagus
a few prawns per person
handful of coriander
   (cilantro) stems and leaves
handful of basil leaves
squeeze of lime juice
25 g (1 oz) salted cashews
steamed rice, lime wedges
   and chilli, to serve

MARINADE
1 teaspoon soy sauce
1½ tablespoons lemon juice
1 clove garlic, crushed
2½ tablespoons olive oil

GREEN CURRY SAUCE
1 tablespoon green curry paste
vegetable oil, for frying
1 x 400 ml (14 fl oz) tin
   coconut milk
2 kaffir lime leaves
1 lemongrass stem, cut into
   lengths and bruised
2 teaspoons fish sauce
juice of ½ lime

Cut the eggplants, capsicums, mushrooms and zucchini into suitable sizes and shapes for barbecuing. Put them all in a large glass or ceramic bowl or dish, along with the sweetcorn, snow peas, spring onions and asparagus.

To make the marinade, combine all the ingredients in a small bowl or jug. Pour most of the marinade over the veg and mix well. Sprinkle with some sea salt, then set aside until you are ready to cook. Wrap the snow peas in foil to make a parcel. Put the prawns in a glass or ceramic bowl, pour over the rest of the marinade and refrigerate until needed.

For the sauce, fry the curry paste in a little vegetable oil in a saucepan over gentle heat until aromatic, then pour in the coconut milk; rinse out the tin with a splash of water and add this as well. Add the kaffir lime leaves and lemongrass and bring to the boil. Set aside to cool.

When it is barbecue time, have all your ingredients flameside, ready to go. Gently reheat the green curry sauce, adding the fish sauce and lime juice.

Place the vegetables that need the longest cooking time on the grill first (eggplants, capsicums and mushrooms), then have the others join them as they go along, ending with the asparagus, which will only need a couple of minutes. Lay the prawns on the grill. Have a large bowl nearby to receive the vegetables and prawns as they are cooked, sprinkling them with snipped coriander stems, some torn basil and lime juice as you go. Place the foil package of snow peas on the grill for just long enough to heat through, making these the final addition to your bowl of veg and prawns.

Gently toss everything together, then pour over the green curry sauce. Cover with coriander leaves and more basil, then sprinkle over the cashews. Serve with rice, lime wedges, and sliced red chilli if you like it hot.

TO TRANSPORT
Decant the curry sauce into a large jar and refrigerate until needed. Gather your vegetables in a basket and your seafood in an airtight container – inside an Esky (cool box), if you have any distance to travel – then away you go.

Hot-smoked salmon with kohlrabi remoulade

Salty–sweet hot-smoked salmon – a whole side of it – is a spectacular dish to serve. Barbecue it at home, or take the doings with you; check first that your host has a barbecue with a lid. Otherwise, just cook the salmon in a very hot (220°C/425°F) oven for about 15 minutes – to check if it is done, make a few surreptitious cuts in the middle with the tip of a small knife. Although you won't get the same smokiness, the fish will still caramelise nicely.

Serves 6

1 x 750 g (1 lb 10 oz) side of
  salmon, skin on, scaled
3 tablespoons vegetable oil
2 tablespoons brown sugar
2 teaspoons sea salt

KOHLRABI REMOULADE
600 g (1 lb 5 oz) kohlrabi
½ green apple, cut
  into matchsticks
60 g (2¼ oz/¼ cup)
  mayonnaise
70 g (2½ oz/¼ cup)
  Greek-style yoghurt
1 teaspoon dijon mustard
1 teaspoon
  wholegrain mustard
1 tablespoon lemon juice
1 tablespoon chopped dill

TO TRANSPORT
Just as nice cold as warm, this fish can easily be cooked at home and carried with ice-packs to a summer lunch. The salmon then keeps on giving, as it will last for up to 3 days in the fridge, ready to find its way into sandwiches, a noodle soup, or rice paper rolls. The remoulade is pretty robust too: it can be dressed in advance, and kept for a few days in the fridge.

About an hour before you want to cook the salmon, find a plate or baking tray big enough to hold the side of salmon. Line it with foil, then rub with 1 tablespoon of the oil. Place the salmon, skin-side down, on the foil. Sprinkle over the sugar and salt and drizzle with the rest of the oil, then use your fingers to massage the sugar and salt into the fish. Cover and leave to cure in the fridge or a cool spot for up to 1 hour.

Meanwhile, fill the smoking box of a barbecue with wood chips or twigs. You can experiment with different sorts of wood. A favourite is twigs and leaves from a pink pepper tree, but you can also use sprigs of bay leaves, rosemary or bought smoking chips. If you don't have a smoking box, wrap your plant material in foil to make a parcel, then pierce it a few times to let the smoke out. Preheat your barbecue to hot, with the smoking box inside.

When the barbecue is nice and hot, and the smoking box is doing its thing, carefully lift the salmon, still on its foil, from the plate or tray and pour off any liquid. Transfer the salmon – still on the foil – to the barbecue, close the lid and cook for 10 minutes. Keep an eye on it, in case any residual oil in the foil catches fire (although it is quite fun/scary when it does!).

Meanwhile, for the remoulade, use a mandoline, box grater or a good old-fashioned knife to create long neat shreds of kohlrabi. Place in a large bowl, along with the apple. Combine the rest of the ingredients to make a dressing, then pour over the kohlrabi and apple and gently toss together.

When the fish is cooked, carefully transfer it to a clean plate and leave to rest for a few minutes. Lift the fish off the foil and serve. If you are careful and a bit lucky, you might be able to keep some nice crispy bits of skin on the fish, but it is often a write-off because it is stuck to the foil. Serve warm, or in a salad.

Cauliflower 'rice' salad

I love rice just as it is, so for most of my life I've seen no need to replace it with anything as daft as a smashed-up cauliflower. But it turns out that smashed-up cauliflower is brilliant. In 2007 Wendy and I did a cooking class with NZ expat chef and notorious brassica-fancier Peter Gordon, during which he assured us that cauliflower could be used in place of rice, but I've only recently run with the idea. To make this a complete meal, serve with roasted eggplant and some yoghurt spiked with garlic.

Serves 4–6

500 g (1 lb 2 oz) cauliflower florets
1 red onion, finely chopped
olive oil, for frying
1 teaspoon mild curry powder, or more to taste
dash of chilli powder – optional
20 g (¾ oz) coriander (cilantro) leaves
20 g (¾ oz) flat-leaf parsley leaves
50 g (1¾ oz) cashews, coarsely chopped
seeds from ½ pomegranate
1 tablespoon mint leaves
juice of ½ lime

TO TRANSPORT
If you are taking the cauliflower rice to someone who might like to eat it warm, stop cooking it just before you add the water, to keep the cauliflower firm. Pack it up in a bowl, but keep the cashews, herbs and pomegranate separate. Reheat the cauliflower gently in a pan, then add the extras.

First, work out how you are going to get your cauliflower looking like little grains of rice. The gold standard is to use a powerful food processor: pulse briefly just 5 or 6 times. If you don't have a food processor, you could grate the cauliflower on the coarse side of a box grater, then pass through the result with a knife to chop any larger pieces down to size. I have also had a go at it in several batches with a large knife, chopping like you see chefs doing herbs on the television, but it does tend to fly about everywhere.

Now, in a large pan over low heat, gently fry the onion in a glug of olive oil until it starts to soften. Add the curry powder (and perhaps a dash of chilli, if you like) and fry until aromatic. Now add a tiny splash more oil and the cauliflower, stirring it as if you were making fried rice; this is one dish that doesn't benefit from a lot of oil, so be prudent in your pouring. After a minute or so, add 2 tablespoons of water to give the cauliflower grains a quick steam.

Now, hack away at the coriander and parsley until you have a big pile of finely chopped greenery. Mix this through the warm cauliflower 'rice', along with the cashews. Finish with the pomegranate seeds, mint leaves and lime juice. This is best eaten warm, but is still nice cold as a salad.

A NOTE ON FURTHER PROJECTS
If you are pleased with the cauliflower rice model, then take it from a fellow convert – this is just the beginning. You could use the cauli grains for a modernised kedgeree, that colonial breakfast of rice, smoked fish and eggs. Follow the recipe above, but instead of those herbs and pomegranates, mix through 50 g (1¾ oz) sultanas and 2 teaspoons chopped coriander (cilantro), then garnish with 2 chopped hard-boiled eggs. Finish with lime juice. Chinese fried rice can also benefit from a cauli makeover. Add diced carrots and substitute spring onion (scallion) for the red onion, then stir through peas, strips of omelette and soy sauce at the end.

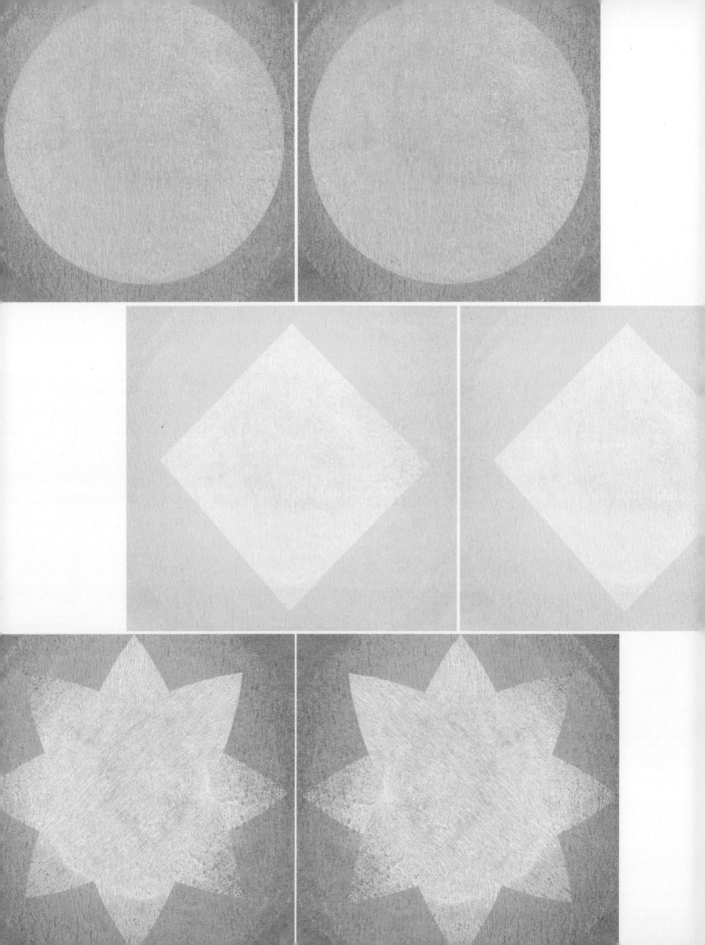

Cakes, tarts and biscuits

Apple tangle cake

Although this cake is quite labour intensive, it's extremely striking and utterly delicious. Crunchy, buttery and apple-y all at the same time, it manages to combine all the best attributes of honey crackles and apple strudel. The secret ingredient is brik pastry (aka brick or warka), a fabulous Tunisian invention that can be found in high-end food shops and online. (Be careful of these food websites, by the way: you venture in looking for brik pastry, and half an hour later you stagger out with kataifi, persimmon dust, four tins of chipotle chillies in adobo, a mixed pack of Persian fairy floss, and several costly grams of dehydrated raspberry chips. Don't say I didn't warn you!)

Anyway, this cake went to Joe Hockey's house, back when he was shadow treasurer and renting out rooms in his Canberra house to colleagues. It was a 'Trojan horse' cake really, designed to get the maker into Canberra's most notorious share house, where former Liberal leader Brendan Nelson famously lived for many years in the shed.

Makes 1 x 23 cm (9 in) cake

4 medium–large mixed apples, such as granny smith, golden delicious, pink lady
2 tablespoons brown sugar
70 g (2½ oz) unsalted butter, melted
1 x 10-sheet packet of brik pastry
100 g (3½ oz) raw sugar
5 brown sugar cubes
small swig o' liqueur – Armagnac would be perfect
50 g (1¾ oz) walnuts, broken into smaller pieces

Peel, core and quarter the apples, then slice roughly into a frying pan. Add the brown sugar and a tablespoon of the melted butter and cook over medium heat for about 8 minutes until the apple slices are a bit soft, but still holding their shape. Pile them into a fine sieve set over a bowl and leave to cool (keep the buttery juices for rice pudding or something else delicious).

Preheat your oven to 180°C (350°F).

Next, you need to cut the pastry to the right shape. Open your packet of brik, which should contain 10 sheets of pastry interleaved with waxed paper. Trace around a 23 cm (9 in) cake tin onto the top sheet of paper. Cut out your circle with scissors – and *voilà*, you have 10 circles of pastry. Keep the scraps of pastry, separating them from their waxy shadows; they will later become the froufrou topping on the cake.

Now butter your 23 cm (9 in) round springform or loose-based cake tin and sit a circle of baking paper in the bottom. (Don't be tempted to use the waxed paper from the brik pastry, for that way disaster lies.)

Diligently removing the paper from the pastry circles as you go, put your first sheet of brik in the bottom of the prepared tin, then paint it generously with melted butter and sprinkle lightly with raw sugar. Repeat with sheets 2 and 3. Bake for about 5 minutes until golden, but not brown.

Recipe continued overleaf...

Cakes, tarts and biscuits

This can be made the night before. Keep the cake and froufrou separate, and transport each in its own tin. On arrival, follow the instructions for assembly; it should require only light titivation. Take a bread knife with you, as a serrated blade is essential to work through the brik pastry. Be aware that this is not a tidy cake. Flakes of pastry and nuts tend to fly everywhere, so it is well suited to the sort of outdoor eating where clean-up means shaking the picnic rug out on the grass.

Add another sheet of pastry to the cake tin and paint it with butter, then add a thin layer of apple slices, leaving a bit of a border around the edge. Soak 1 sugar cube in the liqueur and then crumble this over the top of the apples. Repeat with pastry sheets 5, 6, 7 and 8.

Pastry sheets 9 and 10 are excused from apple duty, but will form a sort of lid for the cake. Holding them in one hand, grab a pair of scissors with the other and make a series of cuts from the outside edge towards the middle. You want to make snips about 8 cm (3¼ in) long, probably about eight in all, until the pastry rounds look a bit like windmill blades. All you're doing here is creating a bit of pastry pizzazz, so it will crinkle up as it bakes. Layer these snipped pastry sheets with butter and sugar just like their predecessors, ending with a final layer of melted butter and sugar on top.

Bake this merry construction for about 15 minutes (or as long as the edges and top can stand without becoming too dark); the longer you can leave it in, the better, but be guided by the colour. You're almost there!

While the main affair is cooking, put together the froufrou. Place your saved pastry scraps in a bowl, pour over the remaining melted butter and sprinkle with the rest of the sugar. Add the walnuts and mix well with your hands. On a lined baking sheet, fashion this mix into a high and decorative tangle about the same diameter as your cake. If your oven is huge, have the froufrou join the cake in the oven, on a separate shelf, for about 6–7 minutes until golden. If you are not blessed with a huge oven, bake the froufrou after the cake.

Once both are cooked and cooled, remove the cake from the tin and lift it gently onto a serving dish or board. Slide the froufrou on top of the cake and sprinkle over any walnuts and pastry pieces that have escaped.

A NOTE ON WORKING WITH BRIK PASTRY
If you like filo, you will love brik pastry. Honestly, this stuff is a dream. It usually has a long fridge life. It's robust, giving you at least 5 minutes before it starts to dry out, and it doesn't tear and flake like filo. But be careful as hell to remove every sheet of paper between the pastry sheets. The paper looks unhelpfully similar to the pastry, so count the sheets of paper in and out like sponges in surgery: you leave one in and it's all over for the patient; same thing with this cake. And don't forget that one sheet of pastry will be left with paper on either side, so it isn't enough to rest easy with the removal of just one sheet each time.

Hummingbird-ish cake

At last, a cake that doesn't need fancy mixers or processors, just a big bowl and a rubber spatula. This version is quite a liberal interpretation of the original hummingbird cake, a banana, pineapple, spice and pecan affair from the southern states of America.

Makes 1 x 20 cm (8 in) cake

1 x 235 g (8½ oz) tin peaches, well drained

100 g (3½ oz) tinned pineapple (about 3 rings), well drained

250 g (9 oz) plain (all-purpose) flour

1 teaspoon ground cinnamon

1 teaspoon ground ginger

1 teaspoon bicarbonate of soda (baking soda)

½ teaspoon baking powder

200 g (7 oz) caster (superfine) sugar

2 large eggs, lightly beaten

200 ml (7 fl oz) neutral-flavoured vegetable oil

2 very ripe, squishy bananas, mashed

50 g (1¾ oz) dried apricots, cut into slivers

100 g (3½ oz) mixed seeds, such as sunflower and pepitas (pumpkin seeds)

CREAM CHEESE ICING

300 g (10½ oz) cream cheese, at room temperature

70 g (2½ oz) unsalted butter, at room temperature

150 g (5½ oz) icing (confectioners') sugar

Preheat your oven to 170°C (325°F). Grease and line three 20 cm (8 in) cake tins. Roughly chop the peaches and pineapple to make a lumpy purée. Sift the flour, spices, bicarbonate of soda and baking powder together into a large bowl, then stir in the sugar. Add the eggs, oil, banana and peach and pineapple purée. Mix until just combined. Fold in the dried apricots and seeds. Divide the mixture among the prepared tins (use scales if you want to be precise) and bake for 15 minutes or until a skewer inserted in the centre comes out clean – as the layers are thin, they'll cook quickly, so keep an eye on them. Leave the cakes to cool on a wire rack.

For the icing, just mix all the ingredients like crazy until you have a smooth, easily spreadable icing.

Assemble the cooled cakes with a thin layer of icing between each one and a final, thicker layer on top.

A NOTE ON TINS AND LAYERS
If you don't have three cake tins, you can bake this cake in two tins, or even one – but as the layers will be thicker, you'll need to increase the cooking time to about 25 minutes for two cakes or 35 minutes for one. With a single cake, just slice it in half horizontally before filling and icing.

TO TRANSPORT
This is a tall and beautiful creature, and it needs careful handling. If you aren't taking it far, then it should be fine resting on someone's knee in the car. If you have a more ambitious trip in mind, or you do not have a car, read on. My advice is to assemble the cake, but leave the final crowning layer of icing to be done at your destination, where you may have to loosen the icing with a teaspoon of hot water. If you need to arrive with a ready-to-go cake, take to some cardboard boxes with a bread knife, taping them together until you have fashioned a kind of high-sided tray to protect your creation. Cover with plastic wrap, first inserting a few toothpicks into the top of the cake to prevent plastic from coming into contact with icing. To hide the pinpricks of damage from the toothpicks, sprinkle the cake with edible flowers.

Cakes, tarts and biscuits

Chocolate beetroot cake

This cake is quick and easy to make . . . if you have a food processor. Apologies to those who don't have that piece of kit. If you have a sturdy blender, that would work too. Either way, what results is a very moist and rich cake, with a delicate, deep red-brown crumb. Even the fussiest of veg-dodgers will be hard-pressed to identify the magic ingredient.

You can use tinned beetroot in this cake if you drain it very well. If starting from scratch, wrap your beetroot in foil and bake it at 160°C (315°F) for an hour or until soft; when it's cool enough to handle, unwrap and slip off the skin.

Serves 8–12

250 g (9 oz) cooked beetroot
300 g (10½ oz) white sugar
150 ml (5 fl oz) vegetable oil
125 ml (4 fl oz/½ cup) buttermilk
2 large or 3 small eggs
225 g (8 oz) plain (all-purpose) flour
1 teaspoon bicarbonate of soda (baking soda)
½ teaspoon baking powder
40 g (1½ oz/⅓ cup) unsweetened cocoa powder

CHOCOLATE ICING
100 ml (3½ fl oz) thin (pouring) cream
200 g (7 oz) milk chocolate (or a mix of milk and dark), grated
100 g (3½ oz) white chocolate

NO BUTTERMILK?
If you don't have buttermilk lying around, don't panic. Soured milk makes a great substitute: add 1½ teaspoons lemon juice to 125 ml (4 fl oz/ ½ cup) full-cream milk. Leave for 2 minutes, then stir.

Preheat the oven to 170°C (325°F). Grease a 30 x 20 cm (12 x 8 in) baking tin and line with a strip of baking paper long enough to overhang the ends.

Purée the beetroot in a food processor until completely smooth. Add the sugar, oil, buttermilk and eggs and blitz again. Sift together the flour, bicarbonate of soda, baking powder and cocoa, then add to the beetroot mix and pulse a few times just to combine. The mix will be quite wet and a nice, very deep reddish colour.

Pour into the prepared tin and bake for around 35 minutes, but start checking at 25 minutes – this cake cooks more quickly than you might expect. It's ready when a skewer inserted in the centre comes out clean.

Leave the cake in the tin to cool completely before icing. If you are going to be serving the cake at home, use the ends of the baking paper lining to carefully lift the cake on to a serving board.

For the icing, gently warm the cream, then remove from the heat and add the milk chocolate. Stir until smooth, then spread over the top of the cake.

While the icing is still warm, melt the white chocolate (see page 188) and scrape it into an icing bag. Pipe lines, as straight as you can, down the length of the cake, then drag a wooden skewer or toothpick through the white lines at right angles. You should end up with a feathered effect. Don't worry if your lines are not straight and your feathering is imperfect – messy is charming. Or you can just pretend your seven-year-old did it.

Let the icing set for an hour or so before serving the cake, cut into squares.

TO TRANSPORT
Couldn't be simpler. Ice the cake in its tin, cut into squares and serve.

Passionfruit polenta cake

Inspired by a Nigella Lawson recipe, this cake is so easy it requires little more than measuring out ingredients. It effortlessly services one's personal obsession with passionfruit (and really, is there ever an end to such things?), one's need for speed and one's guests' appetite for excellence. And, as if it needed further recommendation, this cake is perfect for anyone you know who is coeliac or funny-about-gluten – just make sure you use gluten-free baking powder.

Makes 1 x 20 cm (8 in) cake

150 g (5½ oz) almond meal
100 g (3½ oz) fine polenta (cornmeal)
50 g (1¾ oz) desiccated or shredded coconut
1½ teaspoons baking powder
200 g (7 oz) softened unsalted butter
200 g (7 oz) caster (superfine) sugar
3 eggs, lightly beaten
finely grated zest of 2 lemons or oranges
crème fraîche or cream, to serve

PASSIONFRUIT SYRUP
juice of 1 lemon
pulp from 2 passionfruit
100 g (3½ oz) icing (confectioners') sugar

TO TRANSPORT
This cake keeps well, which makes it a good one to take to people restrained enough to eat it over a couple of days, if you know anyone who falls into that category! It is, however, prone to falling apart if handled too much, so carry it to its destination in its original tin, then transfer to a handsome plate on-site.

Preheat the oven to 180°C (350°F). Grease and line a 20 cm (8 in) springform or loose-based cake tin.

Put the almond meal, polenta, coconut and baking powder in a bowl and mix to combine. Using an electric mixer, cream the butter and sugar together for a few minutes until fluffy. Then, by hand, fold in one third of the combined dry ingredients, followed by a third of the beaten egg. Repeat, mixing well after each addition, until you have a nice smooth batter. Lastly, fold in the lemon or orange zest, then pour the batter into the prepared tin.

Bake the cake for 30 minutes or until you think it's a minute or two shy of being cooked: a skewer won't come out clean, but should have just a few moist crumbs on it. If the edges are looking quite firm, then take it out.

Meanwhile, to make the syrup, heat the lemon juice and passionfruit pulp in a small saucepan over low heat. When it is warm, stir in the icing sugar. You might need to squash some little lumps of icing sugar out. Let the syrup bubble away gently to reduce and thicken slightly.

While the cake is still warm, use a toothpick to make teeny holes all over, concentrating on the edges. Slowly pour the warm syrup over the cake, starting with the edges and working your way towards the middle. It may seem counter-intuitive to pour so much liquid into a perfectly nice looking cake, but it does work out in the end.

Leave the cake to cool to room temperature, then enjoy with some crème fraîche or cream.

Fairy cakes

This is a shout-out for the delicate little fairy cake, a small bite of quality sponge with a dignified structural or decorative element. Now, the thing is, fairy cakes are what Australians ate before the cupcakes landed. Do not even speak to me of the cake pop, because I'm not ready yet, and I may never be ready. Cupcakes have their place, of course. And that place is the United States of America. Be gone with sky-high buttercream and let's bring back the fairy cake.

Makes 8

110 g (3¾ oz) unsalted butter, softened but not sloppy
110 g (3¾ oz) caster (superfine) sugar
110 g (3¾ oz) plain (all-purpose) flour
1 teaspoon baking powder
pinch of bicarbonate of soda (baking soda)
2 eggs, at room temperature
1 tablespoon milk or plain yoghurt – if needed

TO TRANSPORT
Line your favourite vintage cake tin with a clean tea towel and nestle your fairy cakes inside – keep the tin level when carrying, so your fairy cakes don't end up with crushed wings.

Preheat the oven to 180°C (350°F) and line a fairy cake or mini-muffin tin with paper cases.

Start by creaming the butter on low speed in an electric mixer for just as long as it takes you to measure out the rest of the ingredients. We are not striving for light and fluffy today – you just need something pliable enough to let you work in the rest of the ingredients. (You might not even need to bother with this if you are working in a hot kitchen.) Now add the sugar and give it half a minute on low speed to combine. You could also just cream the butter and sugar the old-fashioned way with a wooden spoon and a keen arm.

Sift together the flour, baking powder and bicarbonate of soda, then add to the bowl and mix on low speed for 10 seconds or so until the batter looks mostly combined. Finish it off with a few turns of the wooden spoon. If your batter is very stiff (perhaps because your eggs were small), add a tablespoon of milk or yoghurt to loosen it.

Drop spoonfuls of the batter into the paper cases and bake for about 12–15 minutes or until risen and cooked. Transfer to a wire rack to cool.

You have a whole lot of choices for what to do next . . .

Recipes continued overleaf . . .

Cakes, tarts and biscuits

Butterfly cakes

100 ml (3½ fl oz)
    whipping cream
80 g (2¾ oz/¼ cup)
    strawberry jam or
    passionfruit curd
    (see page 171)
icing (confectioners') sugar,
    for dusting

Whip the cream to firm peaks. Slice the top off each cake with your knife angled inwards, so you are left with a cone-shaped depression. Fill this with jam or curd and whipped cream. Cut the 'hat' of each cake in half to make two 'wings', then sit these on top of the cream. Dust with icing sugar.

Simple icing

100 g (3½ oz) icing
    (confectioners')
    sugar, sifted
hundreds and thousands –
    or other decorations, such
    as a jelly baby, silver ball
    or smartie

Mix the icing sugar with enough hot water (about 3 teaspoons) to make an icing that errs on the side of thin. You're after a consistency that will drop from a spoon. Drizzle the icing over the cooled cakes, giving it a bit of help with the back of the spoon so it spreads in roughly the right directions. Sprinkle hundreds and thousands – or your chosen decorations – on top. Set aside for an hour until the icing has set to crackly.

Lemon icing

100 g (3½ oz) icing
    (confectioners')
    sugar, sifted
3 teaspoons lemon juice
a drop of yellow food
    colouring – optional
crystallised rose or
    violet petals, or other
    edible flowers

Mix the icing sugar with the lemon juice, food colouring (if using) and enough hot water to make a medium–thin icing. Drizzle the icing over the cooled cakes, plant something pretty on top and set aside for an hour until the icing has set to crackly.

Lamington fairy cakes

70 g (2½ oz) icing
    (confectioners') sugar
1 tablespoon cocoa powder
1 teaspoon unsalted butter
2 tablespoons boiling water
45 g (1½ oz/½ cup)
    desiccated coconut

Sift the icing sugar and cocoa powder into a heatproof bowl. Chop the butter into little flecks and melt it in the boiling water, then pour into the bowl and mix well. The icing should be quite runny. While it is still a bit warm, drizzle it over the tops of your fairy cakes. Or, if your cakes have risen enough to peek above the paper cases, you can carefully dunk the tops of the cakes into the chocolate icing while you count to ten. Put the coconut in a small bowl and dip the tops of the cakes to coat, then set your lamington fairy cakes aside for at least an hour.

Apricot slice with lemon icing

I know this slice is a proven traveller because, in the carefree days of our youth, before schools became nut-exclusion zones, Wendy carried it in her lunch box, every other week for 5 years. This is good old-fashioned Australian baking that defies categorisation. Easy to put together, it makes a sturdy yet delicious something for afternoon tea, a cake stall or for cutting into pieces and freezing. I even fancy it would travel well in the post. You could bring it up to date with wholemeal flour and an alternative sweetener, but I prefer this sentimental 1960s version taken directly from Wendy's grandmother's recipe book, with just a slight reduction in the amount of sugar.

Makes 20 small squares

200 g (7 oz) dried apricots,
    finely diced
125 g (4½ oz) unsalted butter
165 g (5¾ oz/¾ cup) raw sugar
90 g (3 oz/1 cup)
    desiccated coconut
300 g (10½ oz/2 cups)
    self-raising flour
80 g (2¾ oz/½ cup) almonds,
    roughly cut in half
125 ml (4 fl oz/½ cup) milk

LEMON ICING
60 g (2¼ oz/½ cup) icing
    (confectioners') sugar
2–3 tablespoons lemon juice

Put the apricots in a deep bowl, pour over enough hot water to just cover and leave for 30 minutes. (As you'll see from the quantity of slowly rehydrating stone fruit you have in front of you, this bake is chiefly fruit, held together by a net of sweet crumbs.)

Preheat the oven to 180°C (350°F) and line a 30 x 20 cm (12 x 8 in) cake tin with baking paper.

Melt the butter and add to the well-drained apricots. In another bowl, combine the sugar, coconut, flour and almonds, then fold into the apricots. Finally, stir through the milk to loosen the mixture. Transfer the batter to the prepared tin – it will be quite solid – and pat down gently. Bake for around 30 minutes, until the top is golden and a skewer inserted in the centre comes out free of any raw batter. Leave to cool on a wire rack.

For the lemon icing, mix the icing sugar with enough lemon juice to make a thin paste. Drizzle over the cooled cake to create a criss-cross pattern. Don't worry if the icing seems too sticky at first – a day in the cake tin will make all the difference. I tried for years to get that delicious crackle of lemon icing on cakes, until I eventually worked out that the only thing separating a gooey icing from a good icing is 24 hours…

This intensely apricot-y treat is best served in small 5 cm (2 in) squares.

TO TRANSPORT
Transport in the tin. Or cut into squares and pile them up in a tin – they will keep their shape quite well.

Chocolate pomegranate cloud cake

This cake has a rich ancestry. A creation of the late Richard Sax, it was then Nigella-fied, becoming quite a hit on the other side of the Atlantic. Originally flavoured with Cointreau and orange zest, here it's wearing a pomegranate fascinator instead. It's a good cake – light but chocolatey, while still somehow pleasing people who aren't mad for chocolate. Easy to get together quite quickly if you have an electric mixer, counter-intuitively it also keeps quite well for a day or so in the fridge. I bet it would also be nice with coffee cream, or a layer of raspberry coulis between the cake and the cream. Or, because I can't think of any dessert that wouldn't be improved by the addition of apricot, a layer of tart apricot compote. This is one of my go-to cakes these days, mostly because even when I am all sugared out, I still have mental space for the pomegranate cloud.

Makes 1 x 23 cm (9 in) cake

250 g (9 oz) dark
  (70% cocoa) chocolate
125 g (4½ oz) unsalted butter
6 large eggs
175 g (6 oz) caster
  (superfine) sugar
300 ml (10½ fl oz) thick
  (double) cream
2 teaspoons icing
  (confectioners') sugar
seeds from ½ pomegranate
  and grated chocolate,
  to decorate
edible dried rose petals –
  optional

Preheat the oven to 180°C (350°F) and line the base of a 23 cm (9 in) springform tin.

Grate or chop the chocolate. Melt the butter in a small saucepan over gentle heat, then remove from the heat and stir in the chocolate – don't stir it too much; if there are any stubborn unmelted bits of chocolate after a few minutes, briefly return the pan to the heat. Once the mixture is smooth and glossy, set aside to cool slightly.

Separate 4 of the eggs and set the whites aside. Using an electric mixer, beat the yolks and the other 2 whole eggs with 75 g (2½ oz) of the caster sugar until really creamy – this may take 3–4 minutes on high speed. Gently fold in the melted butter and chocolate.

In another bowl, whisk the egg whites until they're just frothy, then slowly add the remaining 100 g (3½ oz) of caster sugar while whisking. (Obviously, an electric whisk is almost essential here. Or a tag-team of whisking assistants.) Keep whisking until the mixture holds soft peaks.

Add a big spoonful of the whisked egg whites to the chocolate mixture to loosen it, then carefully fold in the rest, keeping as much air in the mixture as possible. Pour into the prepared tin and bake for about 35 minutes. With this cake, it's better to err on the side of undercooking than overcooking: it should have risen, and then collapsed, and be no longer wobbly around the edges. Don't bother with a skewer, because if it comes out clean, you have overcooked the thing!

Recipe continued overleaf...

Cakes, tarts and biscuits

Leave the cake to cool in the tin; it will sink before your eyes and look as if a meteorite has hit it. But don't worry – we'll be needing a crater to hold all that delicious whipped cream. Speaking of which, whip the cream with the icing sugar (here, err on the side of under-whipped, so it is velvety rather than stiff and grainy).

When the cake is completely cool, run a knife around the edges to loosen the cake from the tin. Then, very, very cautiously, un-spring your cake from the tin and slide it from the base onto a serving plate.

Spread the cream over the top and sprinkle with the pomegranate seeds and grated chocolate. For something really special, dapple your creation with a few rose petals, torn into teeny pieces.

TO TRANSPORT
The safest bet is to carry the cake in its springform tin, then release it at its destination, where you can also proceed to whip the cream and decorate your cake. Individual cakes baked in mini springform tins are a good option if you have any distance to travel.

Persian love cake

I first experienced this cake when Wendy brought it round to my place for lunch. It is a nightingale of a cake: reasonably plain to look at, but its minimal green mosaic of pistachios doesn't even vaguely alert one to the sensory surprise within. Have you ever used a tablespoon of nutmeg in anything before? I haven't, and yet this extreme-sounding prescription is balanced perfectly by the two kinds of sugar and immensely lightened by the yoghurt. This dessert appeared in the first *Kitchen Cabinet* show we ever put to air, a high-kicking episode featuring Amanda Vanstone and Christopher Pyne. In it, I failed to give due credit to the man who invented this cake – Gerard Yaxley, of the late Queensland eatery Qom. I really didn't think anyone would watch the show, but they did, and the cake continues to be a much-requested hit, so I acknowledge him here, with apologies. I have added some lemon zest, but you needn't if you don't want to.

Makes 1 x 26 cm (10½ in) cake

360 g (12¾ oz) almond meal
220 g (7¾ oz/1 cup) raw sugar
220 g (7¾ oz/1 cup, firmly packed) brown sugar
120 g (4¼ oz) unsalted butter, softened
1 tablespoon freshly grated nutmeg
2 eggs, beaten
finely grated zest of ½ lemon
250 g (9 oz) Greek-style yoghurt, plus extra to serve
100 g (3½ oz/¾ cup) pistachio kernels, split
orange segments and rose petals, to serve – optional

Preheat the oven to 180°C (350°F). Grease and line a 26 cm (10½ in) springform cake tin.

Tip the almond meal, both types of sugar and the butter into a bowl and add a pinch of salt. Rub the butter into the dry ingredients until it's evenly incorporated; the mixture should be crumbly, but still able to be squished into a ball.

Split the mixture in half and press one half evenly into the base of your prepared tin. Now turn your attention back to the bowl with the remaining crumbly stuff. Here's where you hook in your nutmeg, eggs, lemon zest and yoghurt. Give the mixture a savage beating with a wooden spoon until it's all smooth and creamy, then pour this into the tin as well.

Arrange the pistachios in a pretty pattern – maybe in a thick ring around the edge, or however else you like – then bake for 40–50 minutes. It's done when the top is deep brown, and the edges look caramelised.

Cool on a wire rack, then carefully remove from the tin. Serve with more yoghurt and a few orange segments, if you like. Rose petals are nice too, if you can get your hands on some unsprayed ones.

TO TRANSPORT
Sit the cake on your favourite cake plate and cover with plastic wrap. Pack into a basket, along with the extra yoghurt and your chosen decorations.

Roasted strawberry ginger cheesecake

The idea for roasting strawberries for a cheesecake is not mine; it's Martha Stewart's. Wendy first spotted the recipe while we were both living in London; she planned to make it for me, but I was so taken with the idea that I jumped the gun and made it myself, thus making this cheesecake another in a long line of culinary ideas I have lifted from Wendy and bolted with. I've varied the crust, though; I like to throw some ginger nuts into the mix to give the whole thing a bit of spice.

I made this for Tanya Plibersek in our first series of *Kitchen Cabinet*. Rather awkwardly, Tanya already knew all about the cheesecake. Turns out I'd made it a while ago for a mutual friend, and Tanya had somehow come by a slice and wanted the recipe. So by the time I bowled up with the thing in a cake tin, Tanya had already made it herself about six times. However, she did a first-rate job of pretending she'd never tasted it before.

Makes 1 x 20 cm (8 in) cake

500 g (1 lb 2 oz)
  strawberries, hulled
3 tablespoons maple syrup
750 g (1 lb 10 oz) cream
  cheese, at room temperature
250 g (9 oz) mascarpone
110 g (3¾ oz/½ cup) caster
  (superfine) sugar
1 vanilla pod (bean), split
  and seeds scraped
2 eggs
icing (confectioners') sugar,
  for dusting – optional

GINGER BISCUIT BASE
125 g (4½ oz) ginger
  nut biscuits
125 g (4½ oz)
  arrowroot biscuits
125 g (4½ oz) unsalted butter

The first thing you need to do is roast your strawberries. Tip them into a baking dish and pour over the maple syrup, then bung into a preheated 100°C (200°F) oven for 1 hour, turning them occasionally and crushing them with a spoon to help things along. When they are ready, they should be dark, jammy and squishy. Scrape absolutely everything from the baking dish into a bowl and leave to cool. Your house will now smell ten kinds of delightful, by the way.

To make the base, increase the oven temperature to 170°C (325°F). Grease a 20 cm (8 in) springform or loose-based tin, and line the base with baking paper. Crush the biscuits – always a messy business, this. A food processor is best, but you can also wrap them in a tea towel and give them a seeing-to with a rolling pin. Add the melted butter to your biscuit crumbs and press the resultant crumbliness into the base of the prepared tin, tamping it down with the base of a drinking glass or similar. Bake for 10 minutes, then remove from the oven and set aside. Reduce the oven temperature to 160°C (315°F).

Next up is the filling, which is dead easy. Using an electric mixer, beat the cream cheese – all of it – until smooth (ignoring the sensation, as you unwrap all those blocks of cream cheese, that you are getting ready for a 1970s dinner party). Add the mascarpone and beat that in too. Ditto the sugar, vanilla seeds and a pinch of salt, followed by the eggs, adding them one by one. By now you should have a smooth, creamy mixture.

Recipe continued overleaf . . .

Remove the beaters and take out about a third of the mixture – this will form the white top layer of the cheesecake. Using a spatula, gently fold the roasted strawberries into the remaining two-thirds of the filling – I like to leave nice streaky ribbons of strawberry through the whole thing, rather than combining everything completely. Pile this onto the base in the tin, smoothing the top with a spatula, then add the reserved third of the mixture and smoothe the surface again.

This delicate cheesecake is best baked in a water bath. Admittedly, this is more fiddly, but it will give you a softer and creamier result. If you don't have one of those excellent springform tins with a fairly infallible silicone seal, wrap your tin, as many times as you can bear, with foil to create a waterproof seal around the bottom. Place the tin in a roomy roasting tin or baking dish, take a deep breath and pour in enough boiling water to come halfway up the sides of your foil-wrapped tin – you need to be pretty confident of your cake tin's seal if you are to embark on this method, even with the foil wrap.

Bake for 1 hour; if the top starts turning brown, tent with some foil. When you remove the cheesecake from the oven, it should still have a slight wobble in the centre. And it will collapse a little bit as it cools. This is *perfectly fine*. When cool, it really needs to go into the fridge for quite a few hours (at least 4) to chill and set.

Dust with icing sugar before serving, if you like.

TO TRANSPORT
Leave the cheesecake in its tin, and transport it thus, then pop it out onto a plate when you get there. I like to serve this as is. Some would advocate cream, but I worry that with a dessert this rich, it could be lethal. Maybe serve with some extra strawberries or a discreet antacid tablet. Up to you.

Blueberry and orange cake with lady grey syrup

In our little bit of the Adelaide Plains, shearing was one of those times of year – like harvest – where, all of a sudden, everyone was incredibly busy round the clock. Country kitchens sprang into action, producing hot meals, sandwiches, tins and tins of biscuits and wicker trays of cake. The recipients, uniform in their blue singlets, would dispatch the treats in between gulps of crazy-strong, overly sugared tea. I don't think those sheds ever saw lady grey tea, or ricotta for that matter, but this cake pays tribute to the spirit of those countless tea breaks and the women who catered them. It even got the nod from Bill Heffernan (a celebrated bushie and tough nut) and minister/aviatrix Sussan Ley.

Makes 1 x 20 cm (8 in) cake

250 g (9 oz) ricotta
150 g (5½ oz) unsalted
    butter, softened
125 g (4¼ oz) caster
    (superfine) sugar
finely grated zest of 3 oranges
3 eggs, separated
25 g (1 oz) almond meal
100 g (3½ oz) plain
    (all-purpose) flour,
    plus extra for sprinkling
2 teaspoons baking powder
dash of milk, if needed
100 g (3½ oz) blueberries,
    fresh or frozen

LADY GREY SYRUP
3 lady grey tea bags
170 ml (5½ fl oz/⅔ cup)
    boiling water
165 g (5¾ oz/¾ cup) caster
    (superfine) sugar
juice of ½ orange

TO TRANSPORT
Carry your cake in an airtight container, with the jar of syrup riding shotgun.

Preheat the oven to 180°C (350°F). Grease a 20 cm (8 in) springform or loose-based cake tin and line with a circle of baking paper. Tip the ricotta into a fine sieve set over a bowl to drain while you make a start on the cake.

Using an electric mixer, cream the butter and sugar until light and creamy, then beat in the zest, followed by the egg yolks, one at a time. Add the ricotta and whisk again – the mixture should be quite fluffy. Fold in the almond meal, then sift in the flour and baking powder, mixing to combine.

In another bowl, whisk the egg whites with a pinch of salt to medium peaks. Take a critical look at the consistency of your cake mixture: if it seems too stiff to gently accommodate the whisked egg whites, stir in a dash of milk to loosen it. Now carefully fold in the egg whites.

Put your blueberries in a bowl and sprinkle with a scant teaspoon of flour (this will help to stop them from sinking to the bottom of the cake).

Pour half the batter into the prepared tin. Sprinkle over all except a few of the blueberries, avoiding the very edges so the finished cake will have solid walls. Add the rest of the batter and sprinkle with the remaining blueberries, using your finger to push them a little way into the batter.

Bake for 35–40 minutes. It can be tricky to tell when this cake is cooked in the middle. Because it's so moist, a knife will come out clean 3–4 minutes before it is actually cooked, so give it a little extra time in the oven after this, until it has a golden, slightly crisp crust.

Meanwhile, forge your strong three-bag brew in the boiling water. After 5 minutes, transfer the tea to a small saucepan with the sugar and orange juice. Bring to the boil, then let it bubble away for 5 minutes to make a thin syrup. Leave to cool until just warm, then transfer to a serving jug.

Cut the cake into slices, then pour over the syrup when serving.

Chocolate and apricot squares

These are a variation on a cake I took to Peter Garrett's place, a teeny terraced house that seemed, frankly, inadequate for a man of his height. That cake was chocolate with a pomegranate jelly layer; these utilise the apricot 'leather' (see page 162) sold in any Middle Eastern grocery worth its salt. If you can't find it, finely chop the same weight of good-quality dried apricots and reconstitute them with the water and lemon juice until soft before whizzing to a paste in a blender or food processor.

Makes about 24

200 g (7 oz) unsalted butter
200 g (7 oz) dark (70% cocoa) chocolate, broken into small pieces
4 eggs
140 g (5 oz) caster (superfine) sugar
60 g (2¼ oz) plain (all-purpose) flour
1½ teaspoons baking powder
200 g (7 oz) apricot leather
juice of ½ lemon
thin (pouring) cream, to serve

CHOCOLATE GLAZE
175 g (6 oz) dark (70% cocoa) chocolate
85 g (3 oz) unsalted butter
1 tablespoon honey

TO TRANSPORT
Once the chocolate glaze has set hard, these squares are quite robust. Save a few back for yourself, then pack the rest side by side in a tin, lined shoe box or large plastic container. They keep quite well, so feel free to make them the night before they're needed.

Preheat the oven to 170°C (325°F). Grease a 26 x 22 cm (10½ x 8½ in) baking tin and line it with baking paper.

In a small, heavy-based saucepan, melt the butter over low heat, then add the chocolate. Let it sit for about 30 seconds, then take off the heat. Stir until you have something smooth and glossy. Whisk the eggs and sugar in an electric mixer on high until the mixture turns pale and is super-light and fluffy. Sift together the flour and baking powder, then add a tablespoonful at a time to the mixer, combining well between each addition. Now mix in the melted chocolate and butter, then pour the lot into the prepared tin and bake for 20 minutes or so – it's fine for this cake to be a little bit soft inside, so take care not to over-cook it.

While the cake is in the oven, roll up your apricot leather (just like rolling up a newspaper to kill a spider) and, with a sharp knife, cut off tiny little slivers – the thinner, the better. Transfer to a small saucepan, along with 4 tablespoons of water, and melt slowly over low heat, stirring often and using the back of a spoon to break up any lumps. Add a little extra water if you're having trouble getting the apricot leather to dissolve. When it's almost there, add the lemon juice and keep cooking until the mixture is reduced to the sticky but pliable consistency of honey on a cold morning.

Pour this apricot goo in a thick stripe down the centre of your cooled cake (it's okay for it to be a tiny bit warm still), then gently spread it out into an even, quite thick layer. Leave to cool completely.

For the chocolate glaze, simply melt all the ingredients together, then stir in a teaspoonful of cold water and leave to cool slightly.

Cut the cake into 24 neat squares and transfer to a wire rack. Drizzle about a tablespoon of glaze over each square, smoothing it with a palette knife so a little runs down the sides. Leave to set in the fridge (or just in a cool spot if there's no space in the fridge), then serve with cream.

Apple crumble cake

I've had mixed fortunes with apple crumble cakes over the years. I have an image in mind, but have often been jinxed by apples that either don't cook through or sink to the bottom, where they become a mutinous and gluey mass. This cake, though, is the apple crumble cake of my dreams: rich, yeasty-tasting, and reminiscent of the excellent crumble cakes to be scored in the German bakeries of South Australia's Barossa region. Slicing the apples thinly ensures they cook through, and the sour cream makes for a nice rich, dense-ish crumb. And the crumble is . . . well, it's crumble. I defy you not to like it. Plus, it's a doddle to make.

Makes 1 x 23 cm (9 in) cake
300 g (10½ oz/2 cups) plain
  (all-purpose) flour
1½ teaspoons baking powder
1 teaspoon ground cinnamon
½ teaspoon freshly
  grated nutmeg
220 g (7¾ oz/1 cup) caster
  (superfine) sugar
4 apples, peeled and
  thinly sliced
3 eggs
245 g (8¾ oz/1 cup)
  sour cream
125 g (4½ oz) unsalted butter,
  melted and cooled slightly

CRUMBLE TOPPING
100 ml (3½ fl oz) melted
  unsalted butter
150 g (5½ oz/1 cup) plain
  (all-purpose) flour
100 g (3½ oz/½ cup)
  brown sugar
1 teaspoon ground cinnamon
65 g (2¼ oz/½ cup)
  slivered almonds

Preheat the oven to 180°C (350°F). Grease a 23 cm (9 in) springform tin.

Sift the flour, baking powder and spices together into a big bowl, then stir in the sugar. Add the apples and toss them about, so the slices are all separated and coated with flour (this will help them to distribute themselves evenly throughout the batter). In another bowl, whisk together the eggs, sour cream and melted butter. Now, just mix the wet and dry ingredients together thoroughly, then pour the batter into the prepared tin. In a smaller bowl, combine all the crumble ingredients and sprinkle thickly over the top.

Bake the cake for approximately 1 hour; I usually tent the thing with foil at about the half-way mark to prevent the crumble from over-browning. The cake is done when a skewer inserted in the centre comes out clean.

TO TRANSPORT
Leave to cool in the tin for 10 minutes, then pop the cake out and transfer it to whichever attractive receptacle you have on hand. Or you can balance it on your knee on a board in the car while navigating – old-style.

Fruit datschi

Plums might be the most traditional fruit used in this slice in its native Germany, but its bastard descendants found in so many South Australian bakeries are doing very well with apricot and apple. In fact, the datschi will happily take whatever the season has to offer: nectarines, strawberries, peaches, cherries, even tinned fruit. Very transport-friendly, this is also good for a crowd.

I had planned to use plums in the version I took to Bill Shorten's house, but I ran out of plums in my rehearsal version and back-filled with fresh strawberries. It turned out that the ring-in fruit delivered not only a super-tasty result, but also a handy pun ('Strawberry Shorten Cake'), so we went with it. Run your own experiments. You can't go far wrong with this one.

Serves 8 generously

380 g (13½ oz) plain
(all-purpose) flour
175 g (6 oz) white sugar
1½ teaspoons baking powder
40 g (1½ oz) poppy seeds
1 teaspoon ground cinnamon
175 g (6 oz) unsalted butter,
at room temperature, cubed
2 eggs
about 1 kg (2 lb 4 oz)
ripe plums, halved
and stones removed
thin (pouring) cream or
vanilla custard, to serve

STREUSEL TOPPING
150 g (5½ oz/1 cup) plain
(all-purpose) flour
165 g (5¾ oz/¾ cup)
white sugar
100 g (3½ oz) unsalted butter
1 teaspoon vanilla paste
or essence

TO TRANSPORT
This is best taken off-site in its baking tin. Serve directly from the tin, or transfer to a large board.

Blitz the flour, sugar, baking powder, poppy seeds and cinnamon in a food processor for a few seconds. Add the butter and pulse until the mixture looks like breadcrumbs. Add the eggs, one at a time, pulsing to combine between each addition. The consistency will be less dry than a traditional shortcrust pastry, more like a biscuit dough.

Grease a 33 x 22 cm (13 x 8½ in) or similar-sized baking tin and lay a sheet of baking paper along its length, leaving enough paper overhanging the ends to act as handles to lift the cooked datschi from the tin. Scrape the mixture into the middle of the tin and use your fingers to push the dough into all corners – it doesn't have to be perfectly smooth and even.

Preheat the oven to 170°C (325°F).

Place the plum halves, cut side up, cheek by jowl, in smart lines on the base, gently pushing down to embed them slightly in the dough. Cram in as much fruit as you can.

To make the streusel topping, stir together the flour and sugar in a bowl. Melt the butter in a small pan over low heat and mix in the vanilla, then pour a little at a time into the flour and sugar, using a knife to make what might best be described as sandy lumps. Once all the butter is in, use your fingers to work in any final bits of dry flour. Sprinkle the topping over the fruit.

Bake the datschi for about 40 minutes. When it's ready, the streusel topping should be golden in parts and the edges of the base should be quite firm (use your baking-paper handles to carefully lift it out and take a peek). Serve at room temperature with cream or custard.

Honey and fig semifreddo cake

Inspired by a recipe in the Green Kitchen Stories blog, this is Wendy's tribute to Golden North's honey ice cream, one of the most reliable treats of our shared South Australian youth. When you pile it up with figs and drizzle it with honey, it's off-the-charts pretty. This is one of the more challenging cakes to transport, but we managed to get it to senator Nick Xenophon's place with the astute deployment of an Esky (cool box) and some prompt freezer-to-freezer transfer.

Serves 8

200 g (7 oz) hazelnuts, or half hazelnuts and half almonds
7 dried figs, hard stems snipped off, chopped – look for the squishier sort
3 good-quality dates, pitted and chopped
2 tablespoons coconut oil
2 tablespoons sesame seeds
honey and fresh figs, to serve

HONEY SEMIFREDDO
1 whole egg
6 egg yolks
150 g (5½ oz) blue gum honey, or whatever paltry substitute you can muster
300 ml (10½ fl oz) thickened (whipping) cream
150 g (5½ oz) Greek-style yoghurt

TO TRANSPORT
This will happily travel for an hour or so in its tin, tucked inside an Esky (cool box) packed with ice. Promptly transfer to a colder environment at your destination – calling ahead to check there is enough freezer space is a wise precaution . . .

Toast the nuts in a 180°C (350°F) oven for 5–10 minutes, or until most of them are taking on a goldy-brown tinge. Keep an eye on them, as they can quickly burn. Rub the skins off the hazelnuts by wrapping them in a tea towel and agitating furiously. (Don't worry about the almonds – their skins don't seem to taste as bitter as hazelnut skins sometimes do.)

Place the cooled nuts in a food processor and pulse until finely crushed, but not completely ground – there should still be plenty of chunks left. Tip the nuts into a bowl, then add the figs and dates, coconut oil and a teaspoonful of water to the food processor and pulse until the mixture is like a sticky glue. Return the nuts to the food processor, along with the sesame seeds, and pulse until you have something that looks like gravel.

Take a loose-based 23 cm (9 in) round tin and cut out a circle of baking paper to fit the base, then place the lined base on a large sheet of plastic wrap. Lift up the plastic wrap and base then drop it back into your tin, so the base is lined with baking paper and the sides are lined with plastic wrap. Press in the gluey nut mixture and freeze for at least half an hour.

For the semifreddo, put the egg, egg yolks and honey in a double boiler, or a heatproof bowl set over a saucepan of simmering water (make sure the base of the bowl isn't touching the water). As the heat makes it way through, whisk and whisk some more until you have a frothy-textured sabayon – this should take about 5 minutes. Remove from the heat and cool to room temperature. Use this time to whip the cream to stiff peaks.

When the sabayon is cool, gently fold in the yoghurt, then the whipped cream. Pour over the base and freeze for at least 4 hours.

About half an hour before serving, transfer the cake from the freezer to the fridge, so it will soften a little and become nicely sliceable. Drizzle with honey and serve with wedges of fresh fig.

Ginger fluff

This lightest, most delicate of sponges relies on ferocious whisking of the eggs and sugar. If you don't have an electrical device for this, then I suggest you roll up your sleeves, because my old-fashioned recipe book says you need to show it who's boss for 20 minutes. If you lack the machinery or the brute strength, it's probably best to choose another cake to bake, because this really is – as the name suggests – all about the fluffiness. Curiously, this sponge seems to be better the day after making, although it's uncommon for it to survive that long.

Serves 8

3 eggs
110 g (3¾ oz/½ cup) caster (superfine) sugar
60 g (2¼ oz/½ cup) cornflour (cornstarch)
1 tablespoon plain (all-purpose) flour
½ teaspoon bicarbonate of soda (baking soda)
1 teaspoon cream of tartar
1 teaspoon cocoa powder, plus extra for dusting
1 teaspoon ground ginger
1 teaspoon ground cinnamon
1 tablespoon warm golden syrup
200 ml (7 fl oz) thin (pouring) cream
1½ teaspoons icing (confectioners') sugar, plus extra for dusting

Preheat the oven to 180°C (350°F) and line the base and sides of two 20 cm (8 in) cake tins with baking paper.

Crack the eggs into a large bowl and add the sugar. Now whisk away, for as long as it takes to get a pale, very fluffy mousse-like consistency – about 5 minutes in an electric mixer, or 20 minutes at full-throttle if you're relying on elbow grease.

Sift together the cornflour, flour, bicarbonate of soda, cream of tartar, cocoa, ginger and cinnamon not twice, but thrice (trust me, I know this is a faff, but it's worth it), then gently fold into the fluffy egg mixture. Lastly, stir in the warm golden syrup.

Divide the cake batter evenly between the two prepared tins and bake for about 30 minutes, or until the top of the sponge springs back when lightly pressed. Cool on a wire rack.

Meanwhile, whip the cream with the icing sugar until it forms soft peaks. Sandwich the cooled cakes together with the whipped cream, then dust with icing sugar and cocoa to serve.

TO TRANSPORT
This cake is fine to take already-made-up if you aren't travelling far. Otherwise, carry the two layers in their cake tins, whip the cream on-site and assemble just before serving.

Linzer torte

Every supermarket bakery, freezer and biscuit aisle seems to have a version of jam tart, and I must say I find most of them secretly delicious. But nothing beats making your own, especially if you use a fine jam of jewel-like colour and satisfying flavour – my favourites are raspberry and apricot.

This tart went to Jenny Macklin's place for lunch once, where Jenny – then a monstrously powerful Labor minister – was incredibly nice about a) me changing my baby on her bed, b) our filming dragging on until dusk and c) the fact that I turned up with something I described as the 'world's oldest tart'. She was kind enough to smile at all of the above.

Serves 8

200 g (7 oz) almond meal
200 g (7 oz) plain
    (all-purpose) flour
200 g (7 oz) white sugar
200 g (7 oz) cold unsalted
    butter, cut into cubes
1 egg, lightly beaten
175 g (6 oz) good-quality
    raspberry jam
thin (pouring) cream, to serve

TO TRANSPORT
Take your linzer torte in its original baking tin. Wrap it in a large tea towel, like a birthday present, and tuck it into a flat basket for the journey, then transfer it into something more appropriate at the scene.

Line a 35 x 10 cm (14 x 4 in) fluted, loose-based tin with baking paper and lightly grease the sides. Avoids tears later.

Put the almond meal, flour and sugar into a food processor and pulse briefly. Add the cold butter all at once and keep doing that pulsing thing until it looks like the butter is being worked in. Add the egg and pulse . . . pulse . . . pulse until you have a crumbly dough that can be pressed into a ball. You might need to add a tiny bit of cold water.

Press all but a small handful of the pastry into the prepared tin. The good news here is that the dough should be applied quite thickly. It's not one of those anxiety-inducing thin and crispy pastry shells we are after, so no rolling and patching needed. Just take big lumps of dough and press them into the tin with the back of a spoon or your fingers. Once you have a fairly even covering in your tin, put it in the fridge for around 30 minutes.

Preheat the oven to 180°C (350°F), placing a baking sheet in the oven as it heats. On a lightly floured surface, roll out the remaining pastry to a 5 mm (¼ in) thickness, then cut into long ribbons (if you have a fluted pastry wheel, dig it out). Take your pastry shell out of the fridge and add the jam, spreading it out evenly, then criss-cross your pastry ribbons over the tart. This is a crumbly pastry, so expect to have to do quite a bit of patching of the ribbons – happily, fixed ribbons look much neater when cooked.

Bake the tart on the hot baking sheet for 35–40 minutes or until the top is golden and the base is cooked. Don't let the edges get too dark or they'll taste burnt; if the top is browning too quickly, cover loosely with foil.

Let the tart cool in the tin. When you are ready to serve, carefully push the bottom of the tin up and out and slide the tart onto a serving plate or board. Eat at room temperature, possibly with a small amount of cream.

Grape and mandarin tartlets

This is your standard French fruit tart, which would usually have strawberries or other soft fruit on top. But grapes and mandarins taste brighter – and because of the handy self-packaging nature of the grape, it doesn't bleed into the pastry cream or look sad and limp after 20 seconds. You might fear that the red, green and orange will turn out looking like a toddler's snack pack, but artfully arranged, the fruit looks very pretty. By all means, use ready-made sweet shortcrust for these. There is no shame in it. But if you are curious or time-rich, give this tart shell a try. The trick is that it uses vodka to replace some of the water, and because alcohol is less effective at activating the gluten in the flour, the result is a softer-textured pastry. A good thing to know if ever you and your spoon have almost shattered a plate and the table underneath trying to get through a tart base.

Makes 6 tartlets

18 mandarin segments (tinned are perfectly acceptable)
18 seedless red grapes
18 seedless white grapes
3 tablespoons marmalade or apricot jam

SWEET SHORTCRUST PASTRY

175 g (6 oz) unsalted butter, softened
70 g (2½ oz) icing (confectioners') sugar
2 egg yolks
3 teaspoons vodka, mixed with 2 teaspoons cold water
250 g (9 oz) plain (all-purpose) flour

PASTRY CREAM

350 ml (12 fl oz) milk
25 g (1 oz) cornflour (cornstarch)
70 g (2½ oz) caster (superfine) sugar
4 egg yolks – make it 5, if your eggs are small
dash of orange flower water – optional

First, the pastry. Put the butter in a food processor and blitz until smooth, then add the icing sugar and pulse a few times. Add the egg yolks one at a time, pulsing in-between. Add about half the vodka and water mix and pulse a few times. Finally, add the flour, along with the rest of the vodka mix and a pinch of salt, and pulse until just combined. Your pastry might look quite wet, but don't worry. Just gather it together and thump it out onto a benchtop. Don't knead it, but use the heel of your hand to smear it over the surface. Use a dough scraper to re-combine and repeat a few times until you have a perfectly combined dough. Now shape it into a ball, cover with plastic wrap and refrigerate for at least 30 minutes, or up to 2 days.

If you're using bought pastry, you can get back on board now. Lightly grease six 8–10 cm (3¼–4 in) tartlet tins. Cut the pastry into 6 pieces, roll each one into a ball, then flatten into a fat disc. Lightly flour your surface and rolling pin, then roll out the pastry to a circle large enough to line the tartlet tins with a generous overhang all around. Gently coax the pastry into the tins, without trimming the excess, then refrigerate for 30 minutes.

Preheat the oven to 180°C (350°F). Line each tartlet shell with foil, covering the edges of the pastry, and fill with baking beads, uncooked rice or dried beans. Bake for 10 minutes, then remove the baking beads and foil. Sit each tartlet tin on one of the pieces of foil, then curl the foil up and over the rim of the tin to prevent the edges of the tartlet shell from burning.

Recipe continued overleaf...

Cakes, tarts and biscuits

I like nothing better than to arrive at someone's house with a disposable piping bag full of something useful. In this instance, pastry cream. Pack the tartlet shells in an airtight container, pre-sieve the glaze and take it in a little jar (for reheating in the microwave). Find yourself a quiet corner and take out your tartlet shells. Snip the end of the piping bag and pipe in the pastry cream, then artfully arrange the fruit on top and finish with a dab of glaze. Now watch your head, because praise and admiration will be raining down upon it.

Bake for another 7 minutes, but keep an eye on the colour. The tartlet shells will get no further cooking after this, so it's now or never if you want to achieve something crisp and golden. Remove the cooked tartlet shells from the oven and, while they are still warm, use a sharp knife to knock off the excess pastry so it is flush with the edge of the tin. Leave to cool completely. You can make these up to 2 days in advance and store them in an airtight container.

For the pastry cream, put about a third of the milk in a small bowl and mix it with the cornflour to make a thin, smooth paste. Heat the rest of the milk and half of the sugar in a medium saucepan. Meanwhile, in a heatproof bowl, whisk the egg yolks furiously with the rest of the sugar, then add the milk and cornflour paste and keep whisking until smooth. Trickle a little of the hot milk into the egg-yolk mixture, and whisk away. Keep gradually whisking in the hot milk until it has all been incorporated, then tip the lot back into the saucepan. Place over low heat and stir constantly until it reaches a simmer, at which point the pastry cream should thicken. If you're using the orange flower water, stir it in now. Take a piece of greaseproof paper or baking paper and lay it directly onto the surface of the pastry cream to stop a skin forming. Set aside to cool.

For the assembly, take your tartlet shells and spoon some pastry cream into each one. Carefully arrange the mandarin segments and grapes on top.

In a small saucepan, warm the marmalade or jam with 1 tablespoon of water until it is runny, then sieve out the peel to make an (almost) instant glaze. Use a pastry brush to paint each piece of fruit, so it looks shiny and ready for action. But hold your horses. Rest the tartlets (or refrigerate, if it's a hot day) for at least 10 minutes before eating, so the glaze can set.

Cranberry Anzac biscuits

The Anzac is the ultimate special-delivery biscuit. Designed to be eggless during the First World War, so it could survive a long sea journey to dear and distant recipients, it is now an unshakeable national favourite. There are ancillary skirmishes over the chewiness or flatness of these things, but no-one seriously thinks they can be made with honey, maple syrup, treacle or any of the other substances that might, under other circumstances, stand in for golden syrup. This version is for a flat, crisp Anzac. It embraces modernity by incorporating dried cranberries. Resist the urge to call them 'Cranzacs'. We did.

Makes about 30

190 g (6¾ oz/2 cups) rolled (porridge) oats
150 g (5½ oz/1 cup) plain (all-purpose) flour
45 g (1¾ oz/½ cup) desiccated coconut
100 g (3½ oz) dried cranberries
125 g (4 oz) caster (superfine) sugar
125 g (4 oz) unsalted butter
125 g (4 oz) golden syrup
1 teaspoon bicarbonate of soda (baking soda)

TO TRANSPORT
Keep in an airtight container is about the only rule. After that, it's up to you. Drop them off to your neighbour, or send them by sea mail to the other side of the world. This is a versatile biscuit.

In a large bowl, mix together the oats, flour, coconut, cranberries and sugar.

Put the butter and golden syrup in a small saucepan over a timid flame and wait until the butter has melted and the golden syrup is very runny, then remove from the heat. Dissolve the bicarbonate of soda in a tablespoon of hot water and add to the golden syrup mixture. Expect to see fizzing. Without a doubt, this is the most pleasing part of the process.

Now mix the bubbling golden syrup mixture into the dry ingredients in the bowl until you have a firm biscuit dough.

Preheat the oven to 160°C (315°F) and line a large baking tray with baking paper.

If you can, it is nice to have all your Anzacs the same size. Wendy found herself an old-fashioned cookie-dough scooper (like a mini ice-cream scoop, with a spring-loaded dough remover) and has never looked back. I use Mum's trusty old double-teaspoon method, where you scoop with one teaspoon and scrape with the other, achieving a wonky sort of quenelle. Either way, leave plenty of room around each ball, because these buggers spread. You will probably only be able to fit six on each tray, and it is for this reason that you need to mark out at least an hour in your diary when you are making these. Unless, of course, you have a *huuuuge* oven and a whole lot of baking trays.

Bake each batch of biscuits for about 10 minutes. They need to be dark golden to achieve the teeth-challenging snap and deeply more-ish taste. Transfer the biscuits, still on the baking paper, to a wire rack to cool – they will crisp up as they cool.

Pineapple and pepper coconut tart

This was inspired by the fondly remembered taste of a pineapple, pepper and coriander tart eaten at Pierre Hermé's patisserie in the Saint-Germain district of Paris. That's the neighbourhood formerly populated by Simone de Beauvoir, Jean-Paul Sartre and almost everyone else who has ever published a decent book. After much simplifying, this version made its way to Barnaby Joyce's then home, in deepest Queensland, thousands of literal and metaphorical miles from its Left Bank roots.

Makes 1 large or 6 small tarts

25 g (1 oz) desiccated coconut
35 g (1¼ oz) almond meal
20 g (¾ oz) icing
    (confectioners') sugar,
    plus extra for dusting
2 egg whites
55 g (2 oz/¼ cup) caster
    (superfine) sugar

PINEAPPLE TOPPING
1 small ripe, sweet pineapple
finely grated zest of ½ lime
8 coriander (cilantro) leaves,
    finely chopped
freshly ground black pepper

COCONUT CUSTARD
2 tablespoons cornflour
    (cornstarch)
55 g (2 oz/¼ cup) caster
    (superfine) sugar
125 ml (4 fl oz/½ cup) milk
200 ml (7 fl oz) coconut milk
2 egg yolks

MARMALADE GLAZE
4 tablespoons marmalade

TO TRANSPORT
If you are planning to put together this folly away from home, take the base, topping, custard and glaze separately and assemble at your destination.

In a large bowl, mix together the coconut, almond meal and icing sugar. In another bowl, whisk the egg whites to snowy, soft peaks, adding the caster sugar little by little as you whisk until you have a glossy meringue. With a flexible spatula, delicately fold the egg white into the coconut mixture.

Line a baking tray with baking paper. Use a piping bag if you want to be neat, but otherwise just smooth the mixture onto the prepared baking tray: if you're making one large tart, shape it into a shallow bowl; if you're making individual tarts, form it into several little nests. Dust lightly with icing sugar and leave to rest for 10 minutes.

Meanwhile, preheat the oven to 70°C (150°F). Cook the tart shells for 25 minutes until they are pale golden – they should be set on the outside, but still gooey in the middle. Leave to cool.

For the topping, peel and core the pineapple, then cut into small wedges and drain in a sieve for a few minutes, pressing gently every now and again to draw out some of the juice. Transfer the drained pineapple to a non-reactive bowl and add the lime zest, coriander and a turn or two of black pepper. Allow to macerate for at least 20 minutes.

Now for the custard. Mix the cornflour, sugar and a pinch of salt in a heavy-based saucepan. Place over low heat, whisk in the milk and heat until almost (but not quite) boiling. Whisk in the coconut milk and egg yolks and keep whisking until the custard thickens and starts to look alarmingly like thick wallpaper paste – this should happen fairly quickly. (If the pasty colour offends you, try adding a few drops of yellow food colouring.) Remove from the heat.

Assembly! Spread the custard generously over the tart base, then cover with the pineapple. In a small, heavy-based pan over low heat, bring the marmalade to the boil, then let it cool slightly before painting it over the pineapple. Leave the glaze to cool, then serve right away.

2D gingerbread houses

Once, for my daughter Audrey's class party, I promised to bake anything she liked. Her request? Gingerbread replicas of all her classmates. In the end, I got away with piping initials and faces on gingerbread figures. Here, with these 2D gingerbread houses, you get the fun of decorating, without the headache of gingerbread architecture, and there is no better housewarming gift than a gingerbread portrait of the new dwelling. Here comes the get-out clause: if you really aren't artistic, or you're in a hurry, just use a round biscuit cutter or drinking glass to cut some circles and pipe a border and the new house number onto the cooked and cooled biscuits. I have a set of 'numbers' biscuit cutters that have produced countless contributions to kids' birthday parties over the years. If you know someone turning three, then rocking up with a plate of gingerbread 3s – painted with a stripe of lemon icing and dipped in hundreds and thousands – is always a welcome move.

Makes about 12

410 g (14½ oz/2¾ cups) plain (all-purpose) flour
1 teaspoon ground ginger
½ teaspoon ground cinnamon
½ teaspoon fine salt
125 g (4 oz) unsalted butter
55 g (2 oz/¼ cup) brown sugar
260 g (9¼ oz/¾ cup) golden syrup
½ teaspoon bicarbonate of soda (baking soda)
1 egg, beaten
1 teaspoon white vinegar

ICING
1 egg white
185 g (6½ oz/1½ cups) icing (confectioners') sugar
1 teaspoon lemon juice

TO TRANSPORT
Carefully pack into a tin or container, cushioning any more delicate architectural features with tissue paper.

Sift the flour, ginger, cinnamon and salt into a mixing bowl. Melt the butter, sugar and golden syrup in a medium saucepan, then add the bicarbonate of soda and allow it to fizz. When the fizzing subsides, add to the dry ingredients and stir well, then add the egg and vinegar and keep mixing to make a firm dough. Shape the dough into a fat rectangle, then roll it out to a 5 mm (¼ in) thickness – don't go too thin, or your biscuits will be delicate and hard to handle.

Now comes the arty part. Mock up an outline of the house on a piece of paper, and roughly sketch what you intend to pipe with icing. Keep it simple, but remember that some distinguishing characteristics, like cast-iron lacework or rows of roof tiles, will identify the house, and are repetitive and easy. Tend towards the larger size. Two or three bold 10 x 7.5 cm (4 x 3 in) biscuits will result in more impact (and fewer meltdowns for the artist) than lots of fiddly little biscuits.

Preheat the oven to 180°C (350°F). Line a baking tray with baking paper. Place your template on the dough and cut around it with a knife. Carefully lift your gingerbread onto the prepared tray and bake for 7–10 minutes or until golden. Leave to cool on the tray while you get going on the icing.

Lightly whisk the egg white until frothy, then mix in the icing sugar and lemon juice to make a smooth icing. Use a tiny nozzle to pipe your designs onto the gingerbread – it's a good idea to get your eye in by practising on a sheet of baking paper first. Let the icing set before serving or transporting.

Mexican wedding biscuits

These biscuits go by a different name and shape in almost every cooking culture. *Rogaliki*, *polvoron*, *kourabiedes*, *vanillekipferl*, Italian butterballs – these are just a few of their aliases. With so many disguises, Biscuit Interpol wouldn't stand a chance. Wendy first encountered them as a ten-year-old during illicit raids on her aunt's pantry. Years later, she strategically made a German friend who sends her these biscuits in the post. They always arrive as a box of crumbs that she eats with a spoon, and very delicious and thoughtful crumbs they are too.

Makes 16

100 g (3½ oz)
  blanched almonds
140 g (5 oz) unsalted butter,
  at room temperature
30 g (1 oz/¼ cup) icing
  (confectioners') sugar,
  plus extra for dusting
165 g (5¾ oz) plain
  (all-purpose) flour

TO TRANSPORT
These are delicate little biscuits, and careful consideration of transport arrangements is required. Small patty pans placed neatly in a tin would work. Otherwise, nestle them closely up against each other in a lined box and carry very carefully to the lucky recipient. Or, like Wendy's German friend Sabine, you could post them to someone far away and just hope for the best.

Preheat the oven to 180°C (350°F). Spread out the almonds on a baking tray and toast them in the oven for 8 minutes or until just starting to turn golden. Watch them carefully, as there is about 30 seconds difference between done and *oh no*!

While this is happening, use an electric mixer to cream together the butter and icing sugar until fluffy. Or, if the butter is soft enough, you can do this by hand – just keep at it until the two are well combined.

Remove the almonds from the oven, and reduce the oven temperature to 160°C (315°F). When the almonds are completely cool, whizz in a small food processor until coarsely ground: aside from a few lentil-sized pieces here and there, we're after the consistency of semolina. Sift the flour into a bowl and stir in the ground almonds, then add this mixture to the butter and sugar, working it in until you have an even-textured crumby mess.

Pat heaped teaspoonfuls of the crumbs into balls and place on a lined but ungreased baking tray – you can pack these guys in pretty tightly, because they don't spread out much during the cooking process. Transfer to the fridge to rest for 15 minutes, then bake for about 15 minutes. We don't want any dark brown edges, just a subtle uniform mellowing of the colour.

Leave the biscuits to cool on a wire rack. Now for the fun part: dip each biscuit in a bowl of sifted icing sugar, then place on a tray. Once they're all dipped, sift even more icing sugar over the top.

Chocolate chip, fruit and nut cookies

These are terrific biscuits for taking as a gift; they have exactly the right degree of chewiness and look impressive in the tin. The secret to their chewiness is the melting together of the brown sugar and butter, which has the additional virtue of sparing the cook the faff of creaming them together. I use dried apricots, macadamias and white chocolate here, but have also had success with dark chocolate, slivered almonds and dried cherries or cranberries – a combination I took along to the ABC election broadcast in 2013, with strong results.

Makes 36

220 g (7¾ oz/1½ cups)
   self-raising flour
70 g (2½ oz/½ cup) plain
   (all-purpose) flour
110 g (3¾ oz/½ cup) caster
   (superfine) sugar
175 g (6 oz) unsalted butter
200 g (7 oz/1 cup)
   brown sugar
1 egg and 1 extra yolk,
   lightly beaten
1 teaspoon vanilla essence
125 g (4½ oz/⅔ cup) dried
   apricots, chopped
120 g (4½ oz/1 cup)
   quartered macadamias
200 g (7¾ oz) white
   chocolate buttons

Sift both flours into a mixing bowl, then stir through the caster sugar. Melt the butter and the brown sugar together in a small saucepan, then pour into the bowl and mix well. Add the beaten egg and yolk, vanilla essence, dried fruit and nuts and combine thoroughly. Allow to cool before stirring through the chocolate buttons.

Preheat the oven to 180°C (350°F). Line a baking tray with baking paper.

Roll the mixture into 3 cm (1¼ in) balls and flatten onto the prepared tray. Bake the cookies for about 10 minutes, whisking them out of the oven when they reach your desired degree of golden-brownness – the darker they are, the crunchier they'll be.

TO TRANSPORT
Store and transport in an airtight tin.

Almond bread

Almond bread is one of the great problem-solvers of the modern kitchen. Need to use up a few egg whites? Problem solved. Need something to scoop up some sort of custardy deliciousness, the construction of which required a series of egg yolks, thus producing the first-mentioned phenomenon? Bob's your uncle. Almond bread combines crunchiness, toastiness, nuttiness and sweetness in a way that accommodates cheese just as nicely as it does a cup of tea. It was common as dirt where Wendy and I grew up. She comes from a family of almond growers, so this recipe (courtesy of her Auntie Bronwyn) comes with impeccable breeding.

Almond bread makes a nice gift (and you can make a gluten-free version too, by substituting the flour with the same amount of gluten-free flour). Make sure you give yourself plenty of time, though; a hurried almond bread is rarely a successful one, as this is one of the few baked goods for which staleness – four days of it – is a prerequisite.

Makes about 40–60 slices

4 egg whites, at
   room temperature
125 g (4½ oz) caster
   (superfine) sugar
125 g (4½ oz) plain
   (all-purpose) flour
125 g (4½ oz) almonds

Preheat the oven to 180°C (350°F). Grease two 23 cm (9 in) log or loaf tins and line them with baking paper.

Using a hand-held whisk, whisk your egg whites with a scant pinch of salt until soft peaks form. Now gradually whisk in the sugar, and things will start to look glossy. Finally, fold in the flour and almonds, then transfer to the prepared tin and bake for 35 minutes or until a skewer inserted in the centre comes out clean.

Let the almond bread cool completely in the tins, then remove and wrap in a clean tea towel. Leave to dry out for 4 days.

When your almond bread is ready for its second baking, preheat the oven to 90°C (190°F). Use a very sharp, non-serrated knife to slice the almond bread as thinly as possible. (If you have an electric knife left over from the 1980s, then dust it off and employ it for this delicate slicing job.) Spread out the slices on baking trays, spacing them so they are not touching, and dry in the oven for about 2½–3 hours or until crisp and starting to colour.

One of the many, many advantages of this wafer-thin treat is that, if stored in an airtight container, it will keep for at least 2 months.

TO TRANSPORT
Anything airtight is the right thing for transporting almond bread. And because of its extraordinary shelf life, it even lends itself to journeys by post.

Almond meringues

Crisp, sweet, nutty: these things don't need much explaining. Perfect for taking to a kids' party (scope the area thoroughly in advance for the nut-sensitive, *obviously*), they can be infantilised in seconds by the addition of food-colouring gel or a couple of tablespoons of cocoa. But you'll be surprised how quickly adults will get through them, too. They need to be stored and transported in an airtight container, and will keep that way for two weeks, it's said, though no-one round here has ever left them uneaten for that long.

Makes 16

150 g (5½ oz) almonds
3 egg whites
200 g (7 oz) caster (superfine) sugar
food-colouring gel or cocoa powder – optional
90 g (3¼ oz/3 cups) cornflakes

Preheat the oven to 160°C (315°F). Run a knife through the almonds a couple of times to chop a few in half – it is fine if there are still whole nuts in there. Now scatter them over a baking tray and give them 8 minutes in the oven to toast, then leave to cool completely. Reduce the oven temperature to 130°C (250°F).

Using an electric mixer, whisk the egg whites and a pinch of salt to stiff peaks. Still whisking, gradually add the sugar; don't be tempted to add the sugar too quickly, or it will knock out too much air from the egg whites. If you would like coloured meringues, you can add a tiny speck of food-colouring gel now. Alternatively, you could beat in 2 tablespoons of cocoa powder for chocolate meringues. (And if you want an impressive, rippled look, take out half the meringue before adding the colouring or cocoa, then lightly swirl it back in afterwards.) When you have a beautifully stiff and glossy meringue, carefully fold in the cornflakes and toasted almonds.

Line a large baking tray with baking paper. Drop teaspoonfuls of almond meringue on the lined tray and cook in the oven until completely dried. This will probably take just over an hour, maybe longer if you are in humid climes. These really work best if you are in a low-humidity environment – like, say, the arid dusty plains of South Australia's mid-north.

TO TRANSPORT
Airtight is the keyword here. Lovely old vintage biscuit tins look beautiful, but rarely give a good seal. If your heart's set on using one, just truss it up with tape once the meringues are inside.

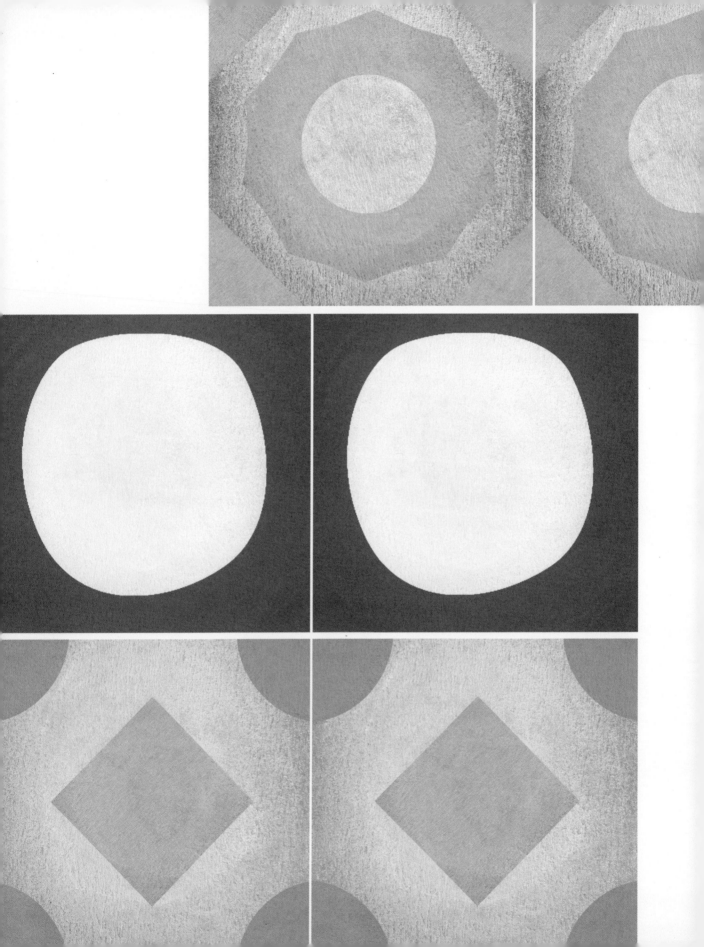

Puddings
and desserts

Bananas Foster vacherin

One day in San Francisco in 2011, Jeremy and I walked into a café with our daughter and ordered a banana milkshake. It was branded as a 'Bananas Foster' milkshake, which meant precisely nothing to me at the time . . . but just a few minutes later, when the milkshake had arrived and I'd tasted it and then wrenched it out of my daughter's innocent fingers and pretty much drunk the whole thing, it meant quite a lot. Bananas Foster is, I subsequently discovered, a Louisiana invention of hellish delight, involving bananas caramelised with butter, sugar, cinnamon and – if you're serious about it, which the milkshake-maker clearly wasn't – some dark rum. It was invented for some customer called Foster in 1951 and galloped on from there.

Here, that same combination of sugar, bananas, dairy and rum is adapted to fill a vacherin, which is like a pavlova that has been encouraged to go a bit soft and chewy. This is good news for those of us who live in tropical climates. The vacherin recipe comes from Wendy's late great-grandma's cookbook, which is full of fancy 1950s party food. It's basically a creamy, blowsy, nutty giant sandwich full of banana and caramel. Mwahahaha.

Serves 8–10

75 g (2½ oz) almonds
4 egg whites
220 g (7¾ oz/1 cup) caster (superfine) sugar
½ teaspoon ground cinnamon
200 ml (7 fl oz) thick (double) cream
2 just-ripe bananas
finely grated chocolate, to serve – optional

CARAMEL SAUCE
110 g (3¾ oz/½ cup) caster (superfine) sugar
60 ml (2 fl oz/¼ cup) thick (double) cream
2 teaspoons spiced rum – optional

Preheat the oven to 180°C (350°F). Scatter the almonds over a baking tray and give them 8 minutes in the oven to toast, then leave to cool completely. Reduce the oven temperature to 140°C (275°F). You could use a food processor to chop the almonds, but I think it is better to go old-style with this and chop them by hand; you want them quite fine with nothing much bigger than a grain of rice.

Whisk the egg whites with a pinch of salt until firm peaks form. Use a big ol' kitchen mixer if you have one, otherwise use a hand whisk. Still whisking, gradually add the sugar and cinnamon until you have a glossy meringue. With a very careful hand, fold in the chopped almonds.

Line a large baking sheet (or two smaller ones) with baking paper, then shape the meringue into two 20 cm (8 in) diameter circles, smoothing the surface – you don't want too much of a peak in the middle. Bake for 1¼ hours or until completely dry, then turn off the oven and leave the meringues inside to cool.

Recipe continued overleaf . . .

Puddings and desserts

With such a long cooking and cooling time, there's really no excuse for not having the caramel sauce ready. In a small heavy-based saucepan, heat the sugar with 2 tablespoons of water over medium heat until it has completely dissolved – you can take the pan by the handle and give it a swirl, but resist the temptation to stir. After about 12–15 minutes, the caramel should start to turn a nice golden brown. Keep a very close eye on it, and when you are happy with the colour, take it off the heat, add a pinch of salt, and leave to cool for a minute or two. Slowly pour in the cream – it will bubble and spit, so be careful – and the rum (if using), stirring constantly.

The assembly is best done a few hours before serving, so the cream can meld with the meringue a bit. Whip the cream until it is just holding its shape – keep it velvety. (For cloud-spotters, think cirrus rather than cumulus.) Place your less-picturesque meringue on a serving plate and cover with two-thirds of the cream. Now slice the banana into thin discs until they cover, and then start to pile up on, the cream. Drizzle a substantial amount of caramel sauce over the bananas and drop spoonfuls of the remaining cream on top. Now place your prettier meringue on top and use both hands to give it a gentle push down, then sprinkle with finely grated chocolate, if using.

TO TRANSPORT

If you want to be super-organised, you can make both the meringues and the caramel sauce a few days in advance, as long as you have an airtight container for the meringues and a clean glass jar for the sauce. This is a surprisingly robust construction, so you could take it in its complete and finished state if staying within local postcodes. Or, if you are travelling long or hot distances, take the meringues and caramel sauce in their respective containers, then whip the cream and construct at your destination, not forgetting to have a couple of hours up your sleeve before serving.

Apricot and pear upside-down puddings

These little puds are incredibly easy to make, and are gluten-free. What's more, I know they travel nicely in their tins, because they once went to Tasmania, to former Greens leader Christine Milne's house. She also took me to a place called The Aproneers, where I first tasted kohlrabi remoulade (see page 100), fuelling my fierce and as-yet-unresolved obsession with that bulbous vegetable.

Makes 8 individual puddings

150 g (5½ oz/1½ cups)
    almond meal
½ teaspoon bicarbonate
    of soda (baking soda)
2 tablespoons brown sugar
1 teaspoon ground ginger
½ teaspoon ground cinnamon
½ teaspoon ground allspice
2 tablespoons vegetable oil
2 small eggs
125 ml (4 fl oz/½ cup)
    apple juice
175 g (6 oz/½ cup) honey
2 pears, cored and thinly sliced
12 x 4 cm (1½ in) squares
    apricot leather or 85 g
    (3 oz/¼ cup) apricot jam
raw sugar, for caramelising –
    optional
cream, to serve

Preheat the oven to 180°C (350°F).

In a large bowl, mix together the almond meal, bicarbonate of soda, sugar, spices and a pinch of salt. In another bowl, whisk the oil, eggs and apple juice. Pour the wet ingredients into the dry and mix until just combined. The batter will look runny, but don't worry – it'll be fine when it's baked.

Grease 8 holes of a muffin tin and line with a small square of baking paper, then squirt in about a teaspoon of honey. Pack a few slices of pear into the bottom of each well, followed by a square of apricot leather or a dob of jam. Pour in the batter, dividing it evenly between the holes, then bake the puddings until browned on top and firm in the middle – this should only take about 15 minutes.

Thanks to your prescient inclusion of baking paper squares, these little beauties should pop right out of the tin after you've left them to cool for 5 minutes.

To finish these puddings, I like to sprinkle a bit of raw sugar on top and caramelise the pear topping under the grill. But don't feel you have to. Serve with cream – clotted, if possible.

TO TRANSPORT
The tactical advantage of these things is that they can travel in their muffin tin. When you get where you're going, just pop them out and reheat them – and perhaps brûlée the tops as discussed, if you're feeling fancy . . .

A NOTE ON APRICOT 'LEATHER'
These puddings owe their tart apricottiness to a square of the Middle Eastern apricot 'leather' or paste that goes under various names, the most common of which is amardeen. You should be able to find it in Middle Eastern shops – but be warned, it's completely delicious.

Rice pudding

It is pointless to write this introduction, really, as the written word is nowhere near capable of conveying the intense comfort of rice pudding. Rice pudding is itself an international language, as it happens; in France it's called *riz au lait*, and in South Asia it's called *kheer*. And its direct translation, in any language, is 'Everything is going to be all right.'

So many things are nice with rice pudding. You could team it with some stewed apples or the spiced cherries on page 186. Or, if it's stone-fruit season, you could halve a couple of yellow peaches, put a dob of butter and some brown sugar in their cavities, and roast them, face-up, at 180°C (350°F) for about 10 minutes.

Serves 6

150 g (5½ oz) short-grain rice,
    such as baldo or arborio
600 ml (21 fl oz) milk
    or almond milk
½ vanilla pod (bean)
3 tablespoons caster (superfine)
    sugar, or more to taste
1 egg yolk

Put the rice into a heavy-based saucepan and pour in 375 ml (13 fl oz/ 1½ cups) of cold water. Bring to the boil, then reduce the heat to low and simmer, uncovered, for 10 minutes. By this time, the rice should be just about cooked, and the water mostly absorbed. Add three-quarters of the milk to the pan, along with the vanilla pod. Bring back to the boil, then immediately turn the heat down to as low as possible, cover and simmer gently for 10 minutes.

Meanwhile, in a bowl, whisk the sugar and egg yolk into the remaining milk. Scoop a couple of large spoonfuls of rice out of the pan into the bowl and whisk to combine. Tip the contents of the bowl into the pan and quickly stir to combine before the egg sets. Keep stirring over low heat for another 5 minutes, then remove from the heat. There will be a seemingly unfeasible amount of liquid left in the pan. Trust me: if you don't have this liquid in reserve, the rice pudding will be gluggy when cold, rather than creamy. Have faith, although I like to panic afresh every time – keeps me young!

Transfer the rice pudding to a bowl and cover with plastic wrap, pressing it directly onto the surface so a skin doesn't form (unless you like skin; and yes, the world is full of strange people). Set aside to cool slightly, then chill in the fridge for at least 2 hours before serving.

TO TRANSPORT
Pack your rice pudding and a serving dish into a basket, and you're all set.

Cherry coconut brownies

David Lebovitz, food blogger extraordinaire and author of *My Paris Kitchen*, nominates kirsch as his fifth most essential baking ingredient (after flour, butter, eggs and sugar), crediting it with bringing out the flavour of not only cherries, but also stone fruit and berries. Of course, it is also rather agreeable for a sneaky half-nip during an afternoon of baking. These brownies were first made out of necessity in a sadly Cherry Ripe-less London, as a homesick homage to the classic Australian chocolate-coated cherry and coconut bar. Made here as individual muffins rather than a whole slab, they are convenient to freeze and can be eaten hot or cold. If cherries aren't your thing, try replacing them with fresh or frozen raspberries, or leaving out the kirsch, coconut and cherries and subbing in a tablespoon of strong espresso and some walnuts. Or go for a pear and walnut combo, or even hazelnut and Frangelico.

Makes 12 brownies

200 g (7 oz) caster (superfine) sugar
2 eggs
100 g (3½ oz) unsalted butter
100 g (3½ oz) chocolate, chopped – I like to use 60 g (2¼ oz) dark and 40 g (1½ oz) milk
100 g (3½ oz) self-raising flour
45 g (1¾ oz/½ cup) desiccated coconut
3 teaspoons kirsch liqueur
120 g (4¼ oz) frozen pitted cherries
cream, to serve – optional

Preheat the oven to 180°C (350°F). Grease a 12-hole muffin tin and line each hole with a square of baking paper.

Use an electric mixer to whisk the sugar and eggs until pale and fluffy.

Melt the butter in a small saucepan over gentle heat. Remove from the heat, stir in the chocolate and wait until it melts into the butter. Fold the butter and chocolate into the eggs and sugar.

Sift in the flour, add the coconut and gently fold everything together. Finally, stir the kirsch and the still-frozen cherries through the batter.

Drop a generous tablespoonful of the batter into each hole, then bake for around 14 minutes – they should still be a bit gooey in the middle. Leave to cool slightly, then gently ease them out of the tin.

Serve at room temperature, or slightly warm. Preferably with cream.

TO TRANSPORT
When cool, transfer your brownies to a large airtight container. If they are destined for a party, give them a minute or two in a 120°C (235°F) oven before serving. However, if you are taking these for general nibbling during a chaotic time in someone's life (say, swotting for exams, or the first weeks with a newborn baby), it's a good idea to deliver them pre-frozen, ready to be popped into the oven or microwave, one or two at a time, during times of acute chocolate-brownie need.

Chocolate choux buns

These are a variation on the cream puff. They borrow from the éclair by wearing a jaunty hat of chocolate ganache, and additionally boast a sprinkling of freeze-dried raspberries. This may strike you as an effeminate dessert, but we took it to the home of Bob Hawke without causing offence; he threw down several during a session of intensive putting practice on his rooftop putting green. In any event, making choux buns is, counter-intuitively, quite a muscular exercise. I always feel, after beating those eggs into the dough, as though I've just finished some sort of super-circuit with Bob Carr. But then, I am an incredible weakling. If, after all that exertion, you don't feel up to piping, just use a spoon to shape the choux dough into rounds.

Makes about 24
100 g (3½ oz) plain
   (all-purpose) flour
85 g (3 oz) unsalted
   butter, cubed
3 small eggs, or 2 large ones,
   at room temperature
freeze-dried raspberries,
   to decorate – optional

PASTRY CREAM
500 ml (17 fl oz/2 cups) milk
4 egg yolks
60 g (2¼ oz) caster
   (superfine) sugar
20 g (¾ oz) plain
   (all-purpose) flour
20 g (¾ oz) cornflour
   (cornstarch)

CHOCOLATE GANACHE
200 ml (7 fl oz) thickened
   (whipping) cream
10 g (¼ oz) unsalted butter
200 g (7 oz) dark
   chocolate, grated

Sift the flour into a bowl. Then sift again, this time onto a sheet of baking paper (trust me, you'll see how this baking paper comes in handy in just a minute). Then, in a medium saucepan, warm 230 ml (7¾ fl oz) of water with the butter over low heat. When the butter has melted, turn up the heat to bring the liquid to boiling point.

Working quickly, with your wooden spoon at the ready, fold your baking paper in half and use it like a slippery dip to whoosh the flour into the pan, all in one go. Turn off the heat. Now whisk like crazy for about half a minute until the flour is well combined and the dough looks a bit like mashed potato. Turn it out onto a large dinner plate and spread it to the edges; this is to cool it enough to allow the eggs to be added without them becoming scrambled.

Crack your eggs into a jug and whisk briefly.

When the spread-out dough has cooled to about body temperature, return it to the saucepan and add the eggs, little by little, beating well in between each addition. This will be – I warn you – incredibly fatiguing, but worth it. Add as much egg as it takes to achieve a smooth dough that will drop, somewhat gingerly, from a spoon; keep in mind that you'll need to pipe this mixture into balls that will hold their shape. Transfer the dough to a piping bag and chill in the fridge for at least 30 minutes or up to a day.

Recipe continued overleaf . . .

To cook the choux, preheat the oven to 200°C (400°F) and line a baking tray with baking paper. Pipe walnut-sized rounds onto the baking tray, smoothing any rough peaks with a wet finger, preferably yours. Bake the choux buns for 25–30 minutes, or until deep golden – pale and golden is undercooked in this context.

Remove from the oven and pierce the base of each choux bun with a small knife (actually, an oyster shucker is ideal) to create a tiny vent for the steam to escape as it cools. If you're really keen to impress, wiggle in your little finger and scoop out any uncooked dough: a perfectly crisp casing will be your reward. Place the buns upside down on the baking tray and return to the oven for 5 minutes to dry them out. Let the buns cool completely before you ice or fill them.

For the pastry cream, heat the milk to just boiling. Mix the egg yolks with the sugar using an electric mixer (or by hand with as much elbow grease as you can muster) for about a minute, then mix in the flour and cornflour to make a smooth paste. Pour the hot milk into the paste in a slow trickle, whisking, whisking all the while. Tip the mixture back into the pan and stir constantly over low heat until it thickens to the consistency of custard. Leave to cool.

Just before you want to serve the choux buns, use a piping bag to fill them with the pastry cream. For the chocolate ganache, use a double boiler (or a heatproof bowl set over a saucepan of hot water) to gently heat the cream and butter, then add the chocolate and stir very cautiously to combine. Don't overheat the chocolate or the ganache may separate.

Dip the filled buns head-first, up to their shoulders, in the ganache, then sprinkle with freeze-dried raspberries, if using. (Sprinkles or hundreds and thousands would also look nice.) Leave the ganache to set for half an hour before serving.

TO TRANSPORT

If you are transporting these off-site, take the dipped but unfilled choux buns, carefully packed, in a cake tin. Take your pastry cream in a tied-off piping bag and keep it refrigerated for as long as possible. With a delicate touch, so as not to disturb the ganache, fill the choux buns at your destination, just before serving. Under no circumstances fill the buns before departure, or you will have a very soggy experience.

Passionfruit curd

This recipe makes a fair amount of passionfruit curd because I am prescient enough to know that you are going to want to use it in other stuff besides the ginger snaps over the page. The curd will keep for up to two weeks in the fridge, and will find its way onto pancakes, tarts and croissants, in between sponge cakes and biscuits, or even into a pavlova with whipped cream. I took just such a passionfruit pavlova to former prime minister Kevin Rudd's house once. He wasn't much for sweets, as it turned out, but his daughter Jessica loved the curd so much I discreetly left her the jar. If you know someone who feels the same way, a jar of this would be the perfect gift for them.

Makes about 700 g
(1 lb 9 oz/2 cups)
110 g (3¾ oz/½ cup) caster
    (superfine) sugar
4 whole eggs
2 egg yolks
125 g (4½ oz) unsalted
    butter, cubed
pulp from 8 passionfruit,
    strained
juice of ½ lemon

In a heatproof bowl set over a pan of simmering water, whisk the sugar, eggs and egg yolks together until pale.

Now whisk in the butter, cube by cube, and keep whisking over the heat: the butter will melt and the mixture will gradually thicken to a nice, custardy texture.

Finally, whisk in the passionfruit pulp and lemon juice and wait for the curd to thicken up again, then immediately transfer it to a bowl (if using straightaway) or sterilised jars (see page 32), covering the surface with plastic wrap so it doesn't form a skin as it cools.

TO TRANSPORT
Spoon the curd into small screw-top jars, giving them a bonnet of muslin (cheesecloth) tied with string, if you like. Pop in your basket and away you go. Remind the recipient to keep their jar of curd in the fridge, and to eat it within 2 weeks.

Ginger snaps with passionfruit curd

These are like brandy snaps, only I haven't called them brandy snaps because that'll put the fear of god into you. You don't have to roll these or shape them into artful baskets, or do anything else that would threaten to inflict severe burns on your fingertips and thus make you a person of interest to the police. You just leave them as little lacy rounds and your guests can load them up with rum cream, passionfruit curd and the fruits of their choice. Or you can pile them up in little towers. Or tilt the snaps with curd and cream between to make a sort of Sydney Opera House tribute! It is possible to get a bit carried away with this, I'm not going to lie.

A word of warning: dreadful things can happen to brandy snaps and their crunchy variants if they are not kept in a properly sealed container. I took brandy-snap baskets to former trade minister Craig Emerson's place in Brisbane once, in a lovely but draughty vintage tin, and by the time I got there the things were as soft as an Emerson harmony. Lesson learned: sometimes, there is a place for function over beauty, even if it means resorting to snap-lock plastic boxes.

Makes 24

50 g (1¾ oz/⅓ cup) plain (all-purpose) flour
½ teaspoon ground ginger
50 g (1¾ oz) unsalted butter
50 g (1¾ oz) golden syrup
50 g (1¾ oz) brown sugar
finely grated zest and juice of ½ lemon
passionfruit curd (see page 171), to serve
fig, mango, kiwi, passionfruit pulp, pomegranate seeds or berries, to serve

RUM CREAM
300 ml (10½ fl oz) thick (double) cream
2 tablespoons dark rum
2 tablespoons maple syrup

Remain calm. Sift the flour and ginger into a heatproof bowl. Take a saucepan and melt the butter, golden syrup and sugar together until they're bubbling and golden (but not burnt!), then pour into the bowl. Add the lemon zest and juice and stir until smooth. Leave to cool slightly.

Preheat the oven to 180°C (350°F) and line a baking tray with baking paper. Place ½ teaspoon dobs of the mixture on the prepared baking tray, spacing them at generous intervals. (I would aim to do about six at a time on a standard-sized baking tray, as they spread quite a bit; you'll end up with snaps about 5 cm/2 in across.)

Bake for about 6 minutes, keeping an eagle eye on them because there is an extremely small window – more of a porthole, really – between perfectly deep golden brown and just plain burnt. It is okay to keep opening and closing the oven door like an idiot in the closing minute.

Finally: rum cream. Just whisk the cream with the rum and maple syrup until it's at the firm-peak stage.

Serve the ginger snaps slathered with cream and curd and topped with fruit.

TO TRANSPORT
Transport all your bits and bobs in a basket: snaps in an airtight container, curd and cream in separate jars, and the whole fruit, ready to prepare when you get there. Set everything out, then let people 'build their own' . . .

Nutty quince crumble

A word in advance: quinces take a stupid amount of time to cook. This is annoying, granted, but the consolation is that they smell absolutely delicious; try to think of a pot of quinces stewing away on the stove as a five-hour scented candle, plus there's dessert at the end. Now, there are intrepid souls who peel and core their quinces before cooking them. I would like to be one of those people, but I never will be. So I just wash and scrub the quinces until I've got most of the fuzz off their skins, then I boil them; they peel and slice easily once they're cooked. I took this dessert to Tony Abbott's house, about a fortnight before the 2013 election. As a passionate Anglophile, he is partial to a bit of nursery pudding, and I suspected – correctly, as it turns out – that this would hit the spot.

Serves 8

5 quinces
650 g (1 lb 7 oz/3 cups) granulated sugar
1 cinnamon stick
2 star anise
2 strips lemon zest
2 thick slices fresh ginger
5 apples, such as pink lady
125 g (4 oz) unsalted butter
55 g (2 oz/¼ cup) caster (superfine) sugar
70 g (2½ oz/½ cup) plain (all-purpose) flour
1 teaspoon ground ginger
70 g (2½ oz/⅓ cup) brown sugar
45 g (1¾ oz/⅓ cup) slivered almonds
45 g (1¾ oz/⅓ cup) chopped macadamias
40 g (1½ oz /⅓ cup) chopped hazelnuts
thick (double) cream or vanilla ice cream, to serve

TO TRANSPORT
Carry the crumble in its baking dish, and the cream or ice cream in a chiller bag.

Okay: scrub your quinces, then pack into a saucepan that will hold them in a single layer. Add the granulated sugar, cinnamon, star anise, lemon zest and fresh ginger, then pour in 1 litre (35 fl oz/4 cups) of water. Bring to the boil, cover and simmer for about 5 hours, turning the quinces every hour or so; I generally cut them in half at about the 3-hour mark to help things along. Test after about 4 hours, and remove once they are deep-red and soft. When they are cool enough to handle, slip off their skins, then core and slice them. (The quince-cooking liquid should be dark red, sweet and fragrant. It will keep in the fridge for 2 weeks, and is good for perking up muesli and yoghurt or drizzling over ice cream. Don't overlook the possibility of jellying it. A quince trifle would be a nice thing. Just saying.)

While the quinces were cooking, you probably found time to peel, core and slice those apples. Hell, you probably had time to write a slim novella. Now you need to soften the apples to get them up to speed with the quinces. Sizzle 25 g (1 oz) of the butter in a frying pan over low heat, then add the apples and caster sugar. Cook, stirring regularly, for about 20 minutes or until the apples are soft and slightly caramelised.

Preheat the oven to 180°C (350°F) and butter a baking dish. Combine the quince and apples, then put as much into the dish as you need for your preferred depth of fruit. (If you have fruit left over, it will keep in the fridge for up to 2 weeks, ready for adding to your morning cereal.)

In a bowl, mix together the flour and ground ginger, then rub in the remaining butter until the mixture resembles coarse crumbs. Stir in the brown sugar and nuts, then sprinkle the crumble over the fruit. Bake for about 25 minutes until heated through and nicely browned on top. Serve warm, with thick cream. Or vanilla ice cream.

Cranachan

A Scottish classic, cranachan is a brilliant cross between breakfast, dessert and late-night booze-athon. Traditionally made with cream, raspberries, oatmeal and huge squirts of Scotch, I devised this version for Doug Cameron, the Labor senator who is a true Scot in every respect – apart, that is, from his decades-old teetotalism. So I used elderflower cordial instead of Scotch, which turned out to be very tasty. Not that this stopped Cameron from sloshing a large dram of single malt all over my serving, though, which wasn't a bad result. If you want a boozier, more authentic cranachan, just substitute whisky for the elderflower cordial in the cream mixture.

Serves 4

300 g (10½ oz) fresh or
 frozen raspberries
3 tablespoons
 elderflower cordial
1 tablespoon butter
2 tablespoons honey
100 g (3½ oz) rolled
 (porridge) oats
300 ml (10½ fl oz) thickened
 (whipping) cream
1 teaspoon vanilla extract
150 g (5½ oz)
 Greek-style yoghurt

Put the raspberries into a small non-reactive pan with 1 tablespoon of the elderflower cordial. Bring to the boil and cook for 2 minutes, then remove the raspberries with a slotted spoon and set aside. Keep cooking down the juices in the pan until syrupy, about 5 minutes. Leave to cool, then return the raspberries to the syrup.

Now for the Scottish-ish touch – the oats. In a heavy-based frying pan, sizzle the butter and honey together. When they're bubbling away, stir in the oats and then toast, stirring regularly, until the oats are golden brown and getting a bit crunchy. Transfer to a plate and set aside to cool.

While the oats are cooling, whip the cream with the remaining 2 tablespoons of the elderflower cordial (or the same amount of whisky) and the vanilla extract until soft peaks form. Gently fold in the yoghurt. If you are a traditionalist with a horror of yoghurt, just use all cream instead.

To serve, layer the cranachan in glasses or a large bowl: first some raspberries, then some elderflower cream, followed by a layer of toasted oats; repeat, ending with oats.

TO TRANSPORT
When the oats have cooled, you're ready to travel. Pop the crunchy oats in a sealed jar or container. Ditto the cream mixture and the raspberries. Find some tall parfait glasses and long spoons. Pack them carefully, and layer on location. If you can't find parfait glasses, you could always use jars. God knows they're being used for just about everything else. Or serve the whole thing trifle-style, in a glass bowl. Still delicious.

Lemon verbena posset

My mother, Christobel, makes a fabulous lemon cordial with lemon verbena leaves (see page 201), a summer drink that inspired Wendy to create this version of the most old-fashioned of desserts. When Wendy sent the recipe for this dessert, I didn't make it right away. It seemed too simple to be really impressive, plus . . . posset? Doesn't that just remind you of the stuff that babies leave on your shoulder? But then I made it and served it to my colleagues – unfortunately, as we drove along. There was nearly an accident when we discovered just how extraordinary something so simple can taste. And now this is one of my favourite desserts ever, a real crowd-pleaser.

Serves 8

500 ml (17 fl oz/2 cups) thick (double) cream
15 lemon verbena leaves, roughly chopped
110 g (3¾ oz/½ cup) caster (superfine) sugar
80 ml (2½ fl oz/⅓ cup) pink grapefruit juice (from about ½ pink grapefruit)
30 ml (1 fl oz) lemon juice (from about 1 lemon)
1 teaspoon finely grated pink grapefruit zest
almond bread (see page 153) or tuiles, to serve – optional

Put the cream in a small saucepan and add the verbena leaves. Bring to the boil, then remove from the heat and leave to infuse for 30 minutes–1 hour.

In another small, non-reactive saucepan over medium heat, dissolve the sugar in the grapefruit and lemon juices with a teaspoon of water and the zest. Bring to the boil, then remove from the heat.

Gently reheat the infused cream, then slowly pour in the warm syrup, whisking all the while. Strain the posset mixture through a fine sieve into a jug, then pour into eight small glasses or teacups and refrigerate for at least 3 hours before serving. You could put a little almond biscuit or tuile on the side if you were feeling fancy.

A NOTE ON LEMON VERBENA LEAVES

These are most commonly found in the herb section of your local plant nursery or, if you're lucky, in an overgrown corner of yours or a friend's herb garden – just make sure they haven't been sprayed. If you can't get your hands on any, you could try making this with lemon myrtle or lemon balm leaves, or even some lemongrass.

TO TRANSPORT

This is quite a rich little pudding, so you only need a small serve. Cast your thinking net far and wide for everyday items that might be useful to hold small cups or glasses: a plastic seedling tray (scrubbed clean, of course); the cardboard trays intended for carrying takeaway coffees; or the sturdy box that once held your plastic wrap, packed with newspaper in between.

German summer pudding

While schools these days seem to be preparing youngsters for the real world with useful subjects such as economics and Indonesian, both Wendy and I spent many years at high school studying German. There were obvious short-term benefits (the ability to communicate with each other discreetly when our parents were within earshot), as well as longer-term ones (the ability to understand those ads for luxury cars). The other knock-on effect has been lifelong access to the under-appreciated world of German cooking. The Barossa Valley, not far from where we grew up, has determined pockets of ambrosial German-influenced baking. This dish is a mush-together of the northern German summer speciality *rote grutze* with that most English of dishes – summer pudding.

It uses Italian sponge, just to confuse things further. You will notice there is no added sugar, which means it tastes quite tart on its own. However, part of the beauty of *rote grutze* is its slightly challenging taste, and the contrast with the vanilla sauce is delicious. Fresh or frozen fruit work equally well for this; to get the real *rote grutze* taste, you need cherries and redcurrants in the mix, but avoid blackberries if you want to keep a nice red colour, rather than a bruised-looking purple. Don't be tempted to skip the sauce – it really does make the dish.

Serves 8–10

500 g (1 lb 2 oz) mixed berries
    and pitted cherries
125 ml (4 fl oz/½ cup) red wine
125 ml (4 fl oz/½ cup) red fruit
    juice, such as red grape
    or cranberry
175 g (6 oz) savoiardi sponge
    finger biscuits (lady fingers)
100 ml (3½ fl oz) thickened
    (whipping) cream
edible flowers, to decorate –
    optional

VANILLA SAUCE

500 ml (17 fl oz/2 cups) milk
½ vanilla pod (bean),
    split and seeds scraped, or
    1½ teaspoons vanilla paste
2 tablespoons caster
    (superfine) sugar
2 egg yolks

Tip the berries and cherries into a small saucepan with the wine and juice and bring to the boil over medium heat, then turn down to low and simmer gently for 5 minutes. Drain off about half of the liquid into a shallow bowl and leave to cool slightly.

Line a 1 litre (35 fl oz/4 cup) pudding bowl with plastic wrap, making sure there is plenty of overhang. Dip the sponge biscuits into the reserved liquid one or two at a time, letting them soak for a few seconds, then line the walls of the bowl with the soaked biscuits. Once you have covered the walls, make some diagonal cuts in a few soaked biscuits to create 'wedges' and use these to fill in the gaps. Next line the base, again cutting and patching to cover as best you can. Make sure you leave yourself at least four biscuits for the lid.

Now whip the cream to soft peaks, then gently fold into the berries. Carefully pour this mixture into the biscuit-lined pudding bowl: it will seem quite wet, but the lady finger is one thirsty biscuit!

Recipe continued overleaf . . .

Puddings and desserts

Soak the remaining biscuits and use to patch together a lid for your pudding – as this will eventually become the base, it can be as messy and imperfect as you like. If there is any remaining liquid, do your best to pour it onto the ends of the sponge fingers lining the sides. Or prise them ever so slightly from the sides and drop some liquid down there. Fold the overhanging plastic wrap over the pudding, then sit a side plate on top to weight it down. Refrigerate for at least 5 hours, or overnight.

For the vanilla sauce, place 400 ml (14 fl oz) of the milk with the vanilla pod and seeds (or vanilla paste) in a small saucepan over medium heat. Whisk the remaining milk with the sugar and the egg yolks in a heatproof jug or bowl. When the milk is hot, gradually add about half of it to the egg-yolk mixture, whisking constantly, then pour it back into the saucepan. Stir the sauce over low heat until it has thickened slightly. With only 2 egg yolks, it will remain quite liquid – remember this is vanilla sauce, not custard. Leave to cool, then refrigerate.

To serve, put your serving plate on top of the pudding, then summon your courage and invert. Your pudding should pop out onto the plate – but if not, a little tug on the edge of the plastic wrap should release it. Decorate with a few edible flowers, if you have them. Cut into wedges and serve with the chilled vanilla sauce.

TO TRANSPORT
There is no better high-impact dessert to transport than this one. Keep it in its pudding bowl, where it will travel as the ugly duckling. But turn it out on the serving plate and it becomes a beautiful swan. Take the vanilla sauce in a tightly sealed jar, and keep it cool en route with an ice-pack.

Winter pudding

Summer pudding's cool-weather twin, in which such fripperies as berries and edible flowers are forgotten in the serious business of maintaining winter condition. To this end, we will require nuts, chocolate and booze. This pudding, once again, uses savoiardi sponge biscuits, and yes, they are usually marketed as 'lady fingers'. (Stop tittering. How old are you, anyway?) Back to the pud in question: winter pudding has a fluffy heart of rich chocolate mousse, and is primed with coffee and hazelnut liqueur. I can offer a 100 per cent guarantee of this dessert's long-range portability, having taken a version of it, discreetly nestled in its basin, from Sydney all the way to former Labor senator Louise Pratt's place in Perth, on a domestic flight. Apart from having my cake forks confiscated at the airport (which smarts to this day), it went like a dream.

If you're up for it, you can even make a spectacular spiky hat of toffee-tailed hazelnuts. These are easier to make than they look, I promise. Save them for stay-at-home puddings, though, as they won't last for long – once they absorb moisture from the atmosphere, they'll start to droop.

Serves 8–10

125 ml (4 fl oz/½ cup) brewed coffee
125 ml (4 fl oz/½ cup) Frangelico liqueur
1 x 200 g (7 oz) packet savoiardi sponge finger biscuits (lady fingers)
100 ml (3½ fl oz) thickened (whipping) cream
125 g (4½ oz) mascarpone
125 g (4½ oz) smooth ricotta
1 tablespoon honey
175 g (6 oz) dark chocolate, melted and slightly cooled

TOFFEE HAZELNUT FOLLIES
20 hazelnuts
200 g (7 oz) caster (superfine) sugar

Take a pudding basin about 15–18 cm (6–7 in) across and with a capacity of 1 litre (35 fl oz/4 cups) and line it with plastic wrap – this is to avoid embarrassing non-cooperation from your pudding when you reach the happy stage of serving your creation. If you are feeling particularly cautious, use two layers of plastic wrap. Allow yourself some time to wrestle the wrap into the basin, as it can be surprisingly recalcitrant.

In a wide shallow bowl, mix together the coffee and Frangelico. Dunk each biscuit for a few seconds to soften, but don't leave them for too long or they'll disintegrate. Line the bowl with your moistened lady fingers (yes, I know – sorry), saving enough to cover the top of the pudding later.

Next, whip the cream to soft peaks. In another bowl, whisk together the mascarpone, ricotta and honey until light and smooth. Gently fold in the slightly cooled melted chocolate, followed by the whipped cream.

Spoon the chocolate mascarpone mixture into the sponge-finger-lined bowl, then cover with more soaked sponge fingers, followed by another layer or two of plastic wrap. Whack the lot in the fridge, weighted with something heavy-ish (like a saucer with a few tins of beans on top) – you want all the juices to soak into the sponge fingers. Leave it for at least 4 hours, or overnight if you can.

Recipe continued overleaf...

Puddings and desserts

This is your chance to tackle the toffee hazelnut follies. Gently spear each hazelnut with a toothpick. Place 20 strips of masking tape along the edge of your kitchen bench (or a table) and spread some newspaper on the floor underneath to catch the toffee drips.

Now for the toffee. Pour 60 ml (2 fl oz/¼ cup) of water into a heavy-based saucepan over high heat. Add the sugar and give it a quick stir, but desist from any further stirring – this is to avoid the sugar crystallising. Swirl the pan around from time to time to dissolve the sugar and keep the mixture from burning. Once the sugar has completely dissolved, watch the syrup closely, as it can quickly become too dark. When it is a pretty amber colour, remove from the heat and leave for a couple of minutes to cool slightly.

Stand at the ready with your spiked hazelnuts. When the toffee has relaxed to a treacle-like consistency, drag a hazelnut through it, repeating to make sure it is quite thickly coated. Now tape the toothpick to your bench so that the speared hazelnut is hanging over the edge and can slow-drip (like a stalactite) onto the floor – hopefully in the spot where you have placed the newspaper. It's very helpful to have an assistant on the job here, to help with the taping. Please do wear closed-in shoes for this; it is an adventure sport. When the toffee in the pan becomes too stiff to use, give it another minute or so on the heat to bring it back to a workable consistency and keep going. Use scissors to snip off the toffee tails at your desired length.

Expect some failures, and count yourself lucky if you end up with seven or eight good specimens. Don't worry if none of them work out – just run a knife through whatever toffee-hazelnut conglomeration you have amassed and sprinkle this coarse praline on top instead.

To serve, carefully ease out your pudding onto a serving plate and arrange some toffee hazelnut follies on top. You could also add chocolate curls if you are one of those people who can make chocolate curls; if you are not one of those people, then I cannot help you, because neither am I. But this tastes so good that no-one will mind either way.

TO TRANSPORT
This pudding travels best cocooned in its original basin. Make it the night before, take it to your destination, turn it out, decorate, and just wait for the oohs and aahs of appreciation.

Spiced cherry Eton mess

Eton mess is a jumbled-up and quintessentially English debacle of meringue, raspberries and whipped cream, to which I add toasted flaked almonds. I have made endless variations over the years, with mangoes, macadamias and all sorts. I took a cherry Eton mess to Julie Bishop's house once, in recognition of her childhood spent on an Adelaide Hills cherry orchard. But this version has another twist – spiced cherries infused with vanilla, cinnamon and star anise. Streaked through the cream and meringue, the dark-red cherry syrup looks spectacular. Plus, it's the easiest thing to prepare in advance and serve on the spot.

Serves 6

500 g (1 lb 2 oz) fresh pitted cherries or 2 x 420 g (15 oz) tins pitted black cherries, drained, syrup reserved

55 g (2 oz/¼ cup) caster (superfine) sugar

125 ml (4 fl oz/½ cup) rosé wine or cherry juice – if using fresh cherries

juice of ½ lemon

2 long strips orange zest

1 vanilla pod (bean), split and seeds scraped

1 cinnamon stick

2 star anise

1 teaspoon cornflour (cornstarch)

300 ml (10½ fl oz) thickened (whipping) cream

2 tablespoons maple syrup

250 g (9 oz) mascarpone, at room temperature

250 g (9 oz) Greek-style yoghurt

10 meringue nests or 150 g (5½ oz) meringues

100 g (3½ oz) slivered almonds, toasted

Cut the cherries in half. If using fresh fruit, put the cherries in a non-reactive saucepan with the sugar, wine or cherry juice, lemon juice, orange zest, vanilla seeds, cinnamon and star anise. Bring to a simmer and cook for 5 minutes, or until the fruit is soft. Make a paste of the cornflour and a tablespoon of water. Add this to the pan, then bring to the boil and cook, stirring gently, until the liquid thickens. Transfer to a bowl and chill.

If using tinned cherries, put 125 ml (4 fl oz/½ cup) of the syrup in a non-reactive saucepan with the sugar, lemon juice, orange zest, vanilla seeds, cinnamon and star anise. Bring to a simmer and cook for 5 minutes. Make a paste of the cornflour with a tablespoon of water. Add this to the pan, then bring to the boil and cook, stirring constantly, until the syrup thickens. Stir the cherries through the thickened syrup, then transfer to a bowl and chill.

Whip the cream with the maple syrup, mascarpone and yoghurt until it forms soft peaks. Spoon the cream mixture into a large bowl, then break up the meringue into 1–2 cm (½–¾ in) chunks and crumble them over the top. Using a large metal spoon, give the meringues and the cream a few turns to mix, then add the cherries and fold just a couple of times to leave ribbons of syrup and fruit running through the cream and meringue.

Pile the lot on a plate or just serve from the bowl. Sprinkle the almond slivers on top. This may not be entirely traditional, but no jury would convict.

TO TRANSPORT

Take the meringues in their packet, the cream mixture in an airtight container and the chilled cherries in their syrup in another. Don't forget the almonds. You'll also need a bowl big enough for folding, and a big spoon.

Mandarin crème brûlée with spiced citrus salad

I spent a few months in 2012 being completely obsessed with mandarins. Their zest, in particular, is delightful: more floral than orange, and more delicate, yet utterly unmistakable. You name it, I probably grated mandarin zest over it. Some combos didn't work. Mandarin with seafood, for instance – yuck. But some, like this mandarin crème brûlée, worked so well that they made it into the permanent repertoire. And when we went to visit Penny Wong to film our first-ever episode of *Kitchen Cabinet*, this is what I took along.

Serves 8

600 ml (21 fl oz) thin (pouring) cream
200 ml (7 fl oz) milk
75 g (2½ oz) honey
75 g (2½ oz) caster (superfine) sugar
8 egg yolks
zest of 6 mandarins, in long strips
4 tablespoons demerara (or white) sugar

SPICED CITRUS SALAD
110 g (3¾ oz/½ cup) caster (superfine) sugar
2 star anise
4 cardamom pods
2 sticks cinnamon
2 strips lemon zest
3 mandarins (some of those you zested above will do nicely), segmented (see page 34)

TO TRANSPORT
Sit your crème pots in a chiller bag or Esky (cool box), and the spiced citrus salad in a sealed container. Take the sugar and your trusty blowtorch with you.

In a heavy-based saucepan, heat the cream, milk and honey until it's twitching with tiny bubbles, steaming a bit and generally looking fidgety.

Meanwhile, in a heatproof bowl, whisk the caster sugar, egg yolks and mandarin zest thoroughly together. Slowly pour the hot cream into the bowl, while whisking the bejesus out of the mixture – this combination of caution and abuse will prevent you from creating a plate of mandarin scrambled eggs, which would not be nice. Once the custard is smooth, pour the whole lot back into the pan and place over low heat. Stir constantly until it has thickened up nicely. Strain the custard to get rid of the zest, then pour into ramekins or sturdy teacups. Or you could use a shallow dish to make a giant crème brûlée and just share it out when you serve it. Either way, put it in the fridge to chill.

Now for the spiced citrus salad. Put the sugar and 125 ml (4 fl oz/½ cup) of water in a heavy-based saucepan and bring to the boil. Let the syrup bubble for 3 minutes, then reduce to a simmer. Add the spices and lemon zest and cook for another 5 minutes. Remove from the heat and leave to cool. Stir through the mandarin segments, then chill in the fridge.

When the moment comes to serve, sprinkle each crème thickly with sugar. Now deploy your blowtorch, passing the flame gently back and forth over the sugar until it has bubbled its way into brown toffee. If you're in a generous mood, you could allow people to blowtorch their own pots.

Like all other recipe writers, I will advise at this point that it is technically possible to brûlée your crèmes by putting them under a super-hot grill (broiler). But my heart's not really in it. Get yourself a blowtorch – you will never regret it.

Serve your crème brûlées on plates flanked by a little pile of citrus salad. I like to leave the whole spices in, just because they look pretty.

Chocolate mousse with raspberry cream and honeycomb

This delightful confection went to Malcolm and Lucy Turnbull's farm at Scone, in the Hunter Valley of New South Wales, when we were filming the third series of *Kitchen Cabinet*. We took the train partly because it is such a terrific train ride, and partly because my baby daughter Kate, a determined small assistant on that series, firmly refused to travel anywhere by car, which meant we were obliged to explore all manner of transport alternatives. Still, there is no feeling quite like taking a dessert on a train to eat with someone interesting. I would definitely recommend it.

There is no use trying to fix something that isn't broken, so the mousse element here sticks to the traditional and elegant formula: chocolate, eggs and sugar. The fastest way to improve chocolate is by adding raspberries and cream, so I did that. The honeycomb? Well, that is just theatre.

Serves 4

120 g (4¼ oz) chocolate, including at least 80 g (2¾ oz) dark chocolate
4 eggs, separated
1 tablespoon caster (superfine) sugar

HONEYCOMB SHARDS
165 g (5¾ oz/¾ cup) granulated sugar
1½ tablespoons runny honey
1 teaspoon of bicarbonate of soda (baking soda)

RASPBERRY CREAM
100 ml (3½ fl oz) double (thick) cream
½ teaspoon vanilla paste – optional
50 g (1¾ oz) fresh or frozen raspberries

First melt the chocolate. Conventional wisdom has it that you should always melt chocolate in a double boiler or heatproof bowl set over a pan of simmering water. But I would suggest that it isn't absolutely necessary to clatter about with bain maries and the like just to melt a bit of chocolate when you can treat it gently in the microwave (on medium for bursts of 30 seconds) or grate it into a hot pan that has been taken off the heat. Leave the melted chocolate to cool slightly.

Next, whisk the egg whites to firm peaks with a tiny pinch of salt, then slowly add the sugar and keep whisking until you have stiff peaks.

Lightly beat the egg yolks, then add to the slightly cooled chocolate and use a whisk to combine. Gently fold in about a third of the egg whites to the chocolate mixture to loosen it, then fold in the rest to the mixture, retaining as much air as possible. Pour into a serving dish (or small glasses) and leave to set for at least 6 hours, preferably overnight.

With all that waiting for the mousse to be ready, you have acres of time to put together the showy honeycomb shards (pictured overleaf). Line a large baking tray with baking paper. Combine the sugar, honey and 1½ tablespoons of water in a tall, heavy-based pan – use a stockpot, if you have one – and heat until it registers 154°C (310°F) on a sugar thermometer (called the 'cracking stage'). If you don't have a thermometer, test by dropping a little of the syrup into a bowl of cold water and then fishing out the result: if it is still stretchy, keep cooking; if it 'snaps', it is ready.

Recipe continued overleaf . . .

Puddings and desserts

Once you are at temperature, take the pan off the heat and sift in the bicarbonate of soda. Be careful – the mixture is awfully hot and it will foam and rise up the pan. Stir with a wooden spoon (or something else non-conductive) until combined, then quickly pour it onto the prepared baking sheet, getting it as thin as you can and smoothing it out with a spatula. Leave the honeycomb for at least 15 minutes to set. Store in a cool, dry place – but not the fridge, or it will go sticky.

Just before serving (or transporting), make the raspberry cream. Whip the cream and vanilla to soft peaks. Fold through the raspberries, crushing them a little as you go to give pretty red streaks, then spoon over the mousse. Break your honeycomb into shards and use to decorate.

A NOTE ABOUT RAW EGG

You will notice that because we are not doing any cooking of the chocolate mousse, the raw egg will stay, well, raw. So think again if you are catering for people who might be nervous about eating raw egg – that is, pregnant women, the very young, the very old, or anyone who is unwell.

TO TRANSPORT

If you live in a perfect world, you will have collected lots of little glass yoghurt containers or straight-sided jars to decant your mousse into. Otherwise, it is absolutely fine to set everything together in a large bowl and scoop out onto individual plates at your destination. It also feels more pleasingly old school served this way. Don't forget the honeycomb shards.

Macadamia, mango and lemon myrtle trifle

The trifle is the grand old dame of transportable dessert. It lives in glasses or a bowl, which is obviously a tremendous help. The trifle artform is riven with controversy. How much booze is too much? Under what circumstances is jelly forgivable?

In 2011, I took this trifle to Darwin for Nigel Scullion, the idiosyncratic and rather charming Northern Territory senator whose early exploits (getting handcuffed to a pole in St Petersburg during a fishing conference, wearing only his underpants) smoothly gave way to a career as a Cabinet minister. To deal with the exigencies of domestic air travel, I made mini-trifles in swing-top jars, with very satisfactory results. Lemon myrtle perfumes the syrup, which soaks the sponge and does double service as a jelly layer with some mango chunks. (In my book, jelly is frequently forgivable.) Fresh lemon myrtle is excellent, if you can get it. Otherwise, use the powdered stuff – just don't bring it to the boil, or you'll kill the flavour.

Makes 6 individual trifles,
or 1 large trifle

300 ml (10½ fl oz)
  cream, whipped
100 g (3½ oz) macadamias,
  chopped and lightly toasted

SPONGE

4 large eggs – total weight
  250 g (9 oz)
250 g (9 oz) unsalted butter
250 g (9 oz) caster
  (superfine) sugar
250 g (9 oz) self-raising flour

LEMON MYRTLE SYRUP

330 g (11½ oz/1½ cups) caster
  (superfine) sugar
10 lemon myrtle leaves,
  chopped, or 2 teaspoons
  ground lemon myrtle

Ingredients continued overleaf...

First, make your sponge. (Perfectly fine to buy one, of course, but there is something a bit fabulous about the old-fashioned sponge recipe that calls for regimented equal proportions of egg, butter, sugar and flour.) The trick is to weigh your eggs, then weigh out exactly the same quantity of butter, sugar and flour. Cream butter and sugar together, beat in the eggs, then fold in the sifted flour and bingo! Lovingly consign your cake batter to a greased and lined 35 x 25 cm (14 x 10 in) cake tin and bake in a preheated 180°C (350°F) oven for about 25 minutes until golden brown and done-looking – it shouldn't leave any sticky stuff on a skewer when you poke it in its middle. (Don't keep opening the oven and poking to test, though: start testing after 20 minutes, and then only if it's looking very brown.) Let the sponge cool, and try not to worry if it collapses. The great thing about trifles is that it doesn't massively matter.

Now make the syrup. Put the sugar and 750 ml (26 fl oz/3 cups) of water in a small saucepan, then bring to the boil and simmer until reduced by a third. Turn off the heat, add the lemon myrtle and let it steep until completely cooled. Strain the infused syrup through a fine sieve; if you're using lemon myrtle powder, line the sieve with muslin (cheesecloth).

Recipe continued overleaf...

CUSTARD
5 egg yolks
110 g (3¾ oz/½ cup) caster
   (superfine) sugar
300 ml (10½ fl oz) thin
   (pouring) cream
300 ml (10½ fl oz) milk

MANGO JELLY
5 gold-strength gelatine leaves,
   soaked in cold water for
   2 minutes
1 large mango, cheeks diced

Next: the custard. In a heatproof bowl, whisk the egg yolks with the sugar until pale. Heat the cream and milk together in a heavy-based saucepan until just starting to boil. Slowly pour the hot cream into the bowl, whisking ferociously the whole time. Pour the whole lot back into the pan and stir constantly over low heat until the custard thickens. Scrape the custard into a bowl and cover with plastic wrap, pressing it onto the surface to prevent a skin forming.

For the jelly, warm 500 ml (17 fl oz/2 cups) of the lemon myrtle syrup, without letting it boil, then add the squeezed-out gelatine leaves and stir until it has completely dissolved. Lay the diced mango in a shallow dish (I use a rectangular lasagne dish), pour over the jelly and stick it in the fridge until the jelly sets.

Okay – now for the fun bit. First, spoon a layer of mango jelly into your trifle bowl, or cut out rounds of jelly if you're using jars. Then add a layer of sponge; don't be afraid to cut your sponge in half if it is too tall. (Ha! As if sponges ever suffer from anything but flatness.) Soak the sponge layer, using the remaining syrup. Now spoon in some custard, then continue layering in this way until you run out of either ingredients or space.

Pop it all in the fridge to ruminate – overnight is terrific, but at least a few hours is mandatory. To serve, slather with whipped cream and a sprinkling of toasted chopped macadamias.

A NOTE ON GELATINE
I like to use leaf gelatine, as I find it gives better and more reliable results. If you want to substitute gelatine powder, 3 teaspoons should be about right here – but follow the packet instructions for setting 500 ml (17 fl oz/2 cups) of liquid, as gelatine is notoriously variable in its setting strength.

TO TRANSPORT
If you've chosen jars, then pack them in a basket for a short journey, or nestle into an Esky (cool box) if you have further to travel. Take the whipped cream and toasted nuts separately and garnish just before serving.

Muscat and almond jelly

Jelly is appealing on a number of levels: its wobble takes us back to childhood, it looks spectacular and it is eminently transportable. And the world of jelly-making is simultaneously full of opportunity (if you can drink it, you can usually jelly it) and pothole-infested (pop in fresh pineapple or kiwi fruit, for example, and your jelly won't set properly – something to do with enzymes, apparently). This recipe is for a double-layered, boozy jelly that's easy to make and very handsome when served in a stemless wine glass or tumbler. Decorate it with some chocolate curls if you are any good at making them – or not.

Just a note about the gelatine. This recipe assumes you will be using standard gelatine leaves of a strength such that one leaf will set 100 ml (3½ fl oz) of liquid. But, for pity's sake, check the label: if you are using powdered gelatine, or extraterrestrial titanium leaves of remarkable setting power, you'll need to adjust the amount accordingly.

Serves 6

ALMOND JELLY
5 gelatine leaves, or enough
  to set 500 ml (17 fl oz/
  2 cups) liquid
400 ml (14 fl oz) unsweetened
  almond milk
60 g (2¼ oz) caster
  (superfine) sugar
100 g (3½ oz) thick
  (double) cream
1 teaspoon vanilla paste

MUSCAT JELLY
4 gelatine leaves, or enough to
  set 400 ml (14 fl oz) liquid
50 g (1¾ oz) caster
  (superfine) sugar
200 ml (7 fl oz) dark muscat

TO TRANSPORT
This jelly is best presented
in glass to show off its two
layers. Keep small jam jars to
use for transport – or, if you
have one, a set of tea glasses
in a metal frame is perfect.

Start with the almond jelly. Soak the gelatine leaves in cold water for a few minutes to soften (or 'bloom'). Put the almond milk and sugar into a small saucepan over medium heat, stirring to dissolve the sugar, then take off the heat and stir in the cream and vanilla paste. Decant about three-quarters of the almond-milk mixture into a heatproof jug. Wring as much water as you can from the gelatine leaves and drop them into the remaining hot liquid in the pan. Stir until they melt away (this happens almost immediately), then pour the contents of the jug back into the pan and stir to combine. Let the jelly mixture cool for a few minutes before pouring it into your serving glasses. Do this carefully, so you don't get splashes up the sides of the glasses, then refrigerate until set – give it 2 hours or so. (Do not use this time to drink all the muscat, as you will need some for the next layer!)

For the muscat jelly, soak the gelatine leaves in cold water for a few minutes to soften. Heat 200 ml (7½ fl oz) of water in a small saucepan, add the sugar and stir until dissolved. Add the muscat and let it simmer for a moment just to take the edge off the alcohol. Pour almost all of the liquid into a heatproof jug. Wring out the gelatine leaves and add them to the remaining hot liquid in the pan and stir to dissolve. Remove from the heat and return the contents of the jug to the pan, stirring well.

Let the jelly mixture cool for about 5 minutes so it's not too hot when you gently pour it on top of the set layer of almond jelly. Return to the fridge for another 2 or 3 hours until the muscat jelly is set.

Drinks party

Cordials and spritzers

Cordial was a constant of my childhood, and I have since found that, decanted into sterilised bottles (see page 32), it makes an eye-catching gift. Christobel Crabb, a woman who could not tolerate a commercial product if a home-made version was conceivable, hit pay dirt with this lemon cordial in the 1970s. A more recent creation, rhubarb cordial is hard to beat for its glorious pink colour, while pomegranate spritzer makes a great non-alcoholic alternative to the cocktails over the page. Of course, both cordials can also be made instantly grown-up with a squirt of soda water and a splash of vodka.

The best lemon cordial

Makes about 2 litres
(70 fl oz/8 cups)

1.5 kg (3 lb 5 oz) caster
(superfine) sugar
500 ml (17 fl oz/2 cups) lemon
juice – from about 6 lemons
25 g (1 oz) citric acid
finely grated zest of 3 lemons
5 lemon verbena leaves

In a large non-reactive saucepan, dissolve the sugar in 2 litres (70 fl oz/ 8 cups) of water over low–medium heat. Add the rest of the ingredients and bring to the boil, then simmer for 2 minutes. Allow the cordial to cool, then pass through a sieve to filter out the leaves and zest. Carefully pour into sterilised bottles. Store in the fridge and use within 2 weeks.

Dilute with water and serve with lots of ice.

Rhubarb and rose cordial

Makes about 375 ml
(13 fl oz/1½ cups)

400 g (14 oz) trimmed
rhubarb, finely sliced
about 200 g (7 oz) caster
(superfine) sugar
1 teaspoon citric acid
4 drops rosewater

Put the rhubarb into a non-reactive saucepan with 250 ml (9 fl oz/1 cup) of water. Bring to the boil, then reduce to a simmer and cook until the rhubarb is completely soft and squashy, about 10 minutes.

Set a sieve lined with muslin (cheesecloth) over a bowl, then tip in the rhubarb and leave for 10 minutes. Now squeeze the rhubarb pulp firmly to get out as much juice as possible. Weigh the juice and add half that amount of sugar, then pour back into the pan and heat gently until the sugar has dissolved. Stir in the citric acid, then leave to cool completely. Add a few drops of rosewater; its potency varies, so taste as you go.

Pomegranate molasses spritzer

Serves 1

200 ml (7 fl oz) pink
grapefruit juice
100 ml (3½ fl oz) lemonade
100 ml (3½ fl oz) soda water
a little pomegranate molasses
mint leaves and pomegranate
seeds, to serve

Mix together the grapefruit juice, lemonade, soda water and a couple of drops of pomegranate molasses. Dot the inside of a glass with pomegranate molasses before filling it up. Serve with plenty of ice, some mint leaves and pomegranate seeds.

Cocktails

Returning a lawnmower or a cookbook? Dropping in to congratulate your pal on a new job or new house? Take a jug of something fabulous with you. If you're a details person, you could even take an ice bucket and glasses. Though in my experience a cocktail slurped out of a teacup – in the right garden, on the right kind of summer evening – is just as delicious as one out of an approved vessel.

Here are three ideas to get you started. The first is a delightful summer concoction that tastes as good as it looks; the next an ode to the place Wendy and I grew up – a drink that smells like the South Australian mid-north; and the last a tribute to Russian grandmothers everywhere.

Summer passionfruit cocktail

Serves 6–8

70 g (2½ oz) caster
  (superfine) sugar
70 ml (2¼ fl oz) lemon juice
70 ml (2¼ fl oz) Cointreau
pulp from 4 passionfruit
1 bottle of prosecco, chilled

Stir the sugar into the lemon juice, dissolving it as best you can, then add the Cointreau and passionfruit pulp. Divide between the glasses and top up with plenty of ice and the well-chilled prosecco.

The Two Wells

Serves 1

seeds and pulp from
  ¼ cucumber
thin wedge of fennel bulb
splash of gin
tonic water
PINK PEPPERCORN
TINCTURE
100 ml (3½ fl oz) vodka
1 teaspoon pink peppercorns,
  plus extra to serve

For the pink peppercorn tincture, put the vodka and peppercorns into a small clean jar and screw on the lid. Leave in a cool, dark place for 10 days, then scoop out the peppercorns and discard. Once made, the tincture will keep indefinitely, ready for the next time.

Now make up a glass with a lot of ice, the cucumber, the fennel wedge and your splash of gin, fill up with tonic, and then 3–4 drops of the tincture. Drop a few extra peppercorns on top. And breathe deeply.

The Russian grandmother

Serves 1

3 teabags strong black tea
2 tablespoons blackberry
  or black cherry jam
2 shots vodka
ginger ale, mint sprig and
  a dash of bitters, to serve

Steep the teabags in 250 ml (4 fl oz/1 cup) of boiling water for 2–3 minutes. Stir in the jam, then strain and leave to cool before adding the vodka.

Transfer to a tall glass, then top up with ginger ale and serve with a mint sprig, a dash of bitters on the rim of the glass – and plenty of ice, of course.

Christobel's spicy nuts

The secret ingredient in these nuts is curry powder. There – I've said it. I do love a recipe with a secret shame ingredient; there's a salad dressing Wendy and I were obsessed with for about two years that includes a tablespoon of tomato sauce. And curry powder here is absolutely perfect, even though it's part of Australia's cultural cringe.

The late, great Don Dunstan, former premier of South Australia, published his own cookbook while in office, and was especially scathing about curry powder: 'What seems to be accepted kitchen practice in this country is that a curry is a weak stew of meat, sometimes with vegetables and even fruit added to it, and flavoured with two teaspoons of a commercial curry powder,' he wrote. 'Having at an early age been fed with delicious goat and chicken curries at the table of my father's great friend Battan Singh, I carefully avoid these Australian insults to a great cuisine.'

Well, sorry Don. It grieves me to report that these nuts are properly tasty; they are a staple gift item in my mum's repertoire, and I can still remember the first time I tasted them. Crispy, salty, sweet, and with that slightly elusive extra something.

Makes about 900 g (2 lb)

1 egg white
850 g (1 lb 14 oz/about 6 cups) nuts – my current thing is half blanched almonds and half raw cashews
55 g (2 oz/¼ cup) caster (superfine) sugar
2 teaspoons fine salt
1 teaspoon freshly ground black pepper
1 teaspoon curry powder
½ teaspoon ground cumin
½ teaspoon ground cinnamon
½ teaspoon cayenne pepper
pinch of ground cloves

Preheat the oven to 160°C (315°F) and line several baking trays with baking paper.

In a large bowl, whisk the egg white to stiff peaks, then add the nuts and stir through until they're evenly coated. Mix all the remaining ingredients together in a small bowl, then add to the bowl of nuts and stir until every nut is covered in the spice mixture.

Now tip the nuts onto your baking trays, spreading them out in a single layer – this is important, because a crowded nut is a soggy nut, and you want these babies to be *crispy*. If in doubt, grab another tray.

Bake until they are a nice deep golden colour – this should take around 15–30 minutes. As they cool, their spicy coating will set hard and crunchy.

TO TRANSPORT
Once you've given these a thorough sampling, pop them in a sealed container quick-smart – moisture is your enemy here. Packed into jars, spicy nuts make very nice presents. And I am certain even Don Dunstan would've secretly liked them.

Smoked mackerel rillettes

When Wendy and I were both living in London, smoked mackerel formed a large part of our diets. It was inexpensive, smoky and salty – three of our key criteria for edibles at the time. I can't remember which genius thought to add cream cheese, lemon and a sharp blade to the fish, but once it was done, the result was on pretty high exchange rotation between our two flats in Belsize Park. With smoked mackerel harder to come by back in Australia, tinned sardines are an acceptable substitute in this whip-up that is more than just a little bit 1970s.

Makes about 250 g (9 oz)

150 g (5½ oz) cream cheese
2 spring onions (scallions), finely chopped
125 g (4½ oz) smoked mackerel, skin removed
2 tablespoons chopped dill
1 teaspoon horseradish sauce
1 tablespoon finely chopped cornichons
2 teaspoons lemon juice
smoked paprika or finely chopped flat-leaf parsley, to garnish
plain crackers or small toasts, to serve

TO TRANSPORT
The sort of small spring-lidded jar traditionally used to preserve French rillettes would be perfect for this. Serve directly from the jar at destination. Or if you are sticking around for the party, spread the rillettes onto small toasts and sprinkle with finely chopped herbs or paprika, then pass around on your host's fanciest tray.

Take the cream cheese from the fridge an hour beforehand, to let it come to room temperature.

Put the spring onion in a medium bowl with the mackerel, dill, horseradish and cornichons. Use the back of a fork to break up the fish and mash it with the other ingredients until all large lumps are gone. Now add the cream cheese and lemon juice and work through until uniformly distributed.

Alternatively, you can use the small bowl of a food processor (or a small blender). Whizz up the cream cheese and spring onion. If you like a smooth consistency, add the mackerel and whizz some more. If you prefer something a little chunkier (I do), mash the mackerel with the back of a fork and then mix through the cream cheese by hand. Then stir in the dill, horseradish, cornichons and lemon juice.

Transfer your rillettes to a small bowl, and dust with something brightly coloured, like brick-red smoked paprika or bright-green parsley.

Serve with plain crackers, or Melba toasts if you want to keep the Seventies theme going.

Carrot and caraway cheese triangles

When approached by a person bearing a tray of filo triangles, the brain of *Homo cocktailpartius attendus* is conditioned to think of spinach and cheese. And there is nothing at all wrong with spinach and cheese triangles, especially if they also contain dill and mint. In my opinion. But these little triangles may surprise, because they are powered by carrot and caraway, plus a judicious blend of cheeses, as well as the aforementioned dill and mint. Yum. They can be made in advance, ready to take to whichever party you're attending and slip into the oven with minimal inconvenience to the host. What's more, the recipe doubles easily for large gatherings. Perfect.

Makes 18

100 g (3½ oz) cottage cheese
2 small carrots, grated – you
    want about 50 g (1¾ oz)
    grated carrot
100 g (3½ oz) feta
100 g (3½ oz) halloumi, grated
1 teaspoon caraway seeds
1 tablespoon finely chopped
    fresh dill and mint
½ teaspoon dried mint
1 x 250 g (9 oz) packet
    filo pastry
50 g (1¾ oz) butter, melted

TO TRANSPORT
Refrigerate or freeze the triangles. Take to the party uncooked, then surreptitiously slide them into the oven on-site.

Sit the cottage cheese in a sieve over a bowl. Press down lightly, then leave to drain. Place the grated carrot on paper towel and squeeze to dry it slightly. In a large bowl, use the back of a fork to squish the feta, then mix in the carrot, halloumi, caraway seeds and the fresh and dried herbs. All those cheeses are tasty enough, so resist the urge to season with salt – just pepper is fine. Lastly, mix in the drained cottage cheese.

Now lay out 3 sheets of the filo pastry (keeping the rest covered with a damp cloth, so it doesn't dry out), then fold in half lengthways and run a knife up the centre to divide them in two – and *voilà*, you now have 6 long rectangles. Lightly brush the pastry rectangles with melted butter, then fold in half lengthways to make even thinner long rectangles. Brush with more melted butter, then put a teaspoonful of the filling about 3 cm (1¼ in) up from one end of a rectangle, on the right-hand side. Fold the bottom-left corner of the pastry over the filling to make a right-angled triangle. Next, fold along the side adjacent to the right angle, then along the longest side, and so on and so on. Keep going until you get to the other end, then use some melted butter to seal the join. Repeat until everything is used up.

Place the triangles on a baking tray lined with baking paper, then give the tops a last lick of melted butter. At this point, you can either forge ahead with baking the triangles or freeze them, flat on a tray.

When you're ready to cook your triangles, preheat the oven to 200°C (400°F), and bake for 10–12 minutes – or 15–18 minutes if cooking from frozen. When they're done, the tops should be very golden: they need quite a bit of time in the oven to make sure the filling is cooked.

These are best eaten warm, not hot. Straight out of the oven, the cheesy centre is like molten rock. Trust me, I know.

Brazilian cheese puffs (pao de queijo)

Don't ask me how these things work. They just do. Pleasingly crisp on the outside and full of gooey, cheesy chewiness in the middle, these are like gluten-free cheese gougères. Made in a blender using tapioca flour (which is available from health-food shops, Asian grocers and some supermarkets), sometimes you just have to wonder how people stumbled across these formulations, but this one is a winner. Ubiquitous in Brazil, apparently, where they are often eaten at breakfast time. For my money, though, I think they are best with a glass of wine.

Makes 36

125 ml (4 fl oz/½ cup) milk
80 ml (2½ fl oz/⅓ cup) vegetable oil
70 g (2½ oz/¼ cup) plain yoghurt
1 egg
240 g (8½ oz/1½ cups) tapioca flour (arrowroot)
70 g (2½ oz/⅔ cup) finely grated parmesan

Preheat the oven to 180°C (350°F) and oil three 12-hole mini-muffin tins (or make and bake these in batches if you only have one tin).

Put everything apart from the parmesan in a blender and whizz until combined. If you don't have a blender, place the ingredients in a large bowl and get very, very busy with a whisk. When everything looks smooth and combined, stir in the parmesan and a pinch of salt.

Pour the batter into the prepared tins and bake for 15–20 minutes or until golden and crisp. These things are, without doubt, best served hot.

A NOTE ON THE PERILS OF TOO MUCH OF A GOOD THING
Do not be tempted to use large muffin tins for these – you'll end up with too much gooey chewiness in the middle of your cheese puffs and quite possibly risk choking on it. (Can't stop thinking about that annual debacle with the mochi rice cakes in Japan, where hundreds of people are hospitalised from speed-eating glutinous rice cakes each New Year. Dreadful business.)

TO TRANSPORT
While these will cope with a reheat, your best bet is to arrive armed with a jug of the batter and your mini-muffin tins. Commandeer some oven space and cook on the spot. Easy.

White and red soup shots

In Regency times, delicate chilled soups were offered in dainty portions at fancy gatherings, and there is still a solid argument for a classy soup served in teeny-tiny portions. Here are two such soups: one white, one red. Both are perfect for pouring into shot glasses and throwing back in a single gulp at a party, or as a starter for a summer dinner.

White soup

Serves 4 as a starter

200 g (7 oz/¾ cup)
  Greek-style yoghurt
250 g (9 oz) cucumber, peeled
  and chopped
1–2 small cloves garlic, crushed
1 tablespoon lemon juice
½ teaspoon chopped dill
½ teaspoon chopped mint
5–6 edible dried rose petals
pomegranate seeds, sumac
  and shreds of unsprayed
  rose petal, to serve

Whizz the yoghurt, cucumber, garlic, lemon juice, dill, mint and dried rose petals in a blender with a pinch of salt until quite smooth. Keep the soup refrigerated in a jug until party time, then give a stir and pour into small shot glasses or shallow bowls.

When ready to serve, carefully drop a couple of pomegranate seeds on top, then add a light sprinkle of sumac and a few slivers of rose petal.

TO TRANSPORT
A tightly sealed jar for the journey – with a few ice cubes thrown in, if you have any distance to cover. But take a jug too, because I don't like your chances of an accurate pour into shot glasses from something without a spout. Especially if you've got cracking on the drinks already.

Red soup

Serves 4 as a starter

1 tablespoon fish sauce
2 teaspoons rice vinegar or
  white wine vinegar
1 teaspoon sugar
½ clove garlic, finely chopped
200 g (7 oz) watermelon,
  peeled and seeds removed,
  roughly cut into chunks
100 g (3½ oz) ripe and tasty
  tomatoes, cut into chunks
few slivers of fresh chilli or
  a tiny pinch of chilli flakes
1 tablespoon lime juice
crumbled feta, to garnish

Put the fish sauce, vinegar, sugar and garlic in a small saucepan with 2 tablespoons of water and heat until the sugar dissolves. Remove from the heat and leave to cool completely.

Meanwhile, use a blender to whizz up the watermelon and tomatoes. When it looks smooth, add the chilli and 2 tablespoons of the fish sauce mixture and give it 5 more seconds on high power. Strain the soup through a sieve, then add lime juice to taste.

Keep the soup refrigerated in a jug until party time, then give a stir and pour into small shot glasses or shallow bowls. Perch a tiny crumb or two of feta on top of each serving.

Goat's cheese and polenta muffins

The cheesy muffin. Dear god, how I love it. I remember once making a batch for Wendy's daughter's birthday party, and they turned out perfectly: not too dry, not too oily, not too eggy. I must have eaten at least ten. But I just made them by randomly throwing in odds and ends of different cheeses I had in the fridge with a tragically un-recall-able proportion of flour, and I have struggled to recreate that dream muffin on a number of occasions since. Wendy, through her own experimenting, has come up with this rather brilliant technique of incorporating some polenta into a cheesy muffin batter, then poking in a scooped-out cherry tomato filled with goat's cheese. The overall effect is quite jaunty, like a little tomato boat sailing a load of goat's cheese across a puffy polenta sea. It also means you get all the benefits of fresh tomato, without any of the usual sog-factor. Genius. These muffins are also nice without the tomato filling, served warm with soup. Or with just the tomatoes, their seeds left intact, or with feta instead of goat's cheese. Okay, I'm stopping now. Or pine nuts. Right, definitely stopping now.

Makes 48

200 g (7 oz/1⅓ cups) plain (all-purpose) flour
1 tablespoon baking powder
90 g (3¼ oz) polenta (cornmeal)
30 g (1 oz) walnuts
1 teaspoon dried tarragon
60 g (2¼ oz) cheddar, grated
1 egg
170 ml (5½ fl oz/⅔ cup) milk
2 tablespoons vegetable oil
30 ml (1 fl oz) melted butter
24 cherry tomatoes
100 g (3½ oz) soft goat's cheese

TO TRANSPORT
Carry these in their tin. Just before serving, reheat at 120°C (235°F) for a few minutes until barely warm.

Preheat the oven to 180°C (350°F) and grease four 12-hole mini-muffin tins (or make and bake these in batches if you only have one tin).

In a large bowl, combine the flour, baking powder, polenta, walnuts and tarragon, then mix through the cheddar.

In another bowl, whisk together the egg, milk, oil and melted butter as best you can. Now make a well in the middle of the dry ingredients and slowly pour in the wet ingredients, combining as you go. You want to end up with a slightly sticky batter – be careful not to over-mix or your muffins will be tough. Drop a teaspoon of the batter into each hole of the prepared tin.

Cut the cherry tomatoes in half and scoop out the seeds, then push a tomato half, cut-side up, right down into each muffin, so that some of the batter oozes up to form something like a tart case around the tomato. Place about ¼ teaspoon goat's cheese into each tomato 'cup', or whatever it takes to modestly fill it.

Bake the muffins for about 10 minutes, keeping an eye on the edges and turning the oven down if they are browning too quickly.

Walnut and red pepper dip (muhammara)

I'd always roasted my own red peppers for this zippy little drinks-party wonder. But recently, on advice from a fellow muhammara fancier, I tried roasted peppers from a jar. Quite an improvement, it turns out – and this leaves more time for cracking fresh walnuts from their shells, which really does boost the quality. Or doing your hair before guests arrive . . .

Makes about 350 g (12 oz)

225 g (8 oz) roasted red
    capsicums (peppers), from
    a jar or fresh – up to you
2 cloves garlic, crushed
30 g (1 oz/½ cup, lightly
    packed) fresh breadcrumbs
115 g (4 oz/1 cup)
    shelled walnuts
2 teaspoons smoked paprika
2 tablespoons
    pomegranate molasses
olive oil, chopped coriander
    (cilantro) and pitta crisps
    (see page 56) or water
    crackers, to serve

Put the peppers and garlic into the small bowl of a food processor (or a small blender) and pulse until chopped in a chunky kind of way. Add the breadcrumbs and pulse some more, just to combine.

Next, toss the walnuts around in a hot frying pan for a minute or so, until they start to smell nice, then tip them out onto a plate. Give the smoked paprika a quick tour of the hot pan (stay with it – you don't want it to burn) and, as soon as it starts to smell toasty, add it to the processor.

When the walnuts are cool enough to handle, rub off any obvious bits of skin, then add to the processor and blitz until smooth. Lastly, when the dip looks uniform and well blended, pulse in the pomegranate molasses.

Transfer to a serving dish, drizzle with olive oil and sprinkle with coriander. Serve with plain pitta crisps or water crackers.

TO TRANSPORT
The good news is that muhammara tastes even better the next day, and can be kept in an airtight container in the fridge for up to 4 days – but I bet it won't last that long. Transport in a glass jar or ceramic container (the colour will stain plastic). Serve in a shallow bowl, surrounded by pitta crisps or crackers.

Quail eggs with two dipping salts

Okay – I know. Quail eggs. But I'm obsessed with the little bastards. I love the way they look, with their mottled shells. And when you peel them, the insides of the shells are a perfect blue. Quail eggs remind me of the miniature-food phase I went through years ago, the insane culmination of which was miniature Scotch eggs, made with a fishcake mixture wrapped around quail eggs.

This recipe couldn't be easier to make and serve. You can boil the quail eggs and grind up the salt mixes in advance, then simply serve the eggs whole in a bowl for guests to peel and dip. An important additional consideration: one quail egg will occupy one child for about 5 minutes.

Serves 6–8

16 quail eggs, or as many as you can get your mitts on

SESAME AND CUMIN SALT
2 tablespoons sesame seeds
1 tablespoon cumin seeds
1 tablespoon rock salt

NORI AND SESAME SALT (FURIKAKE)
1 sheet toasted nori
2 tablespoons white sesame seeds
1 tablespoon black sesame seeds
1 tablespoon dried ground red shiso
pinch of sea salt

First, boil your quail eggs for 3 minutes. Use a timer to be exact because every second counts here. On the knocker of 3 minutes, plunge the eggs into a large bowl of cold water to stop them cooking.

For the sesame and cumin salt, put the sesame and cumin seeds into a small frying pan and toast for 5 minutes, or until the sesame seeds are golden and the cumin seeds fragrant. Tip into a mortar and pestle with the salt and grind to a fine powder.

For the nori and sesame salt, use scissors to snip the nori into the tiniest pieces you can manage, then simply mix with the remaining ingredients.

Serve the dipping salts in small bowls alongside the eggs.

A NOTE ON FURIKAKE
You can often find pre-mixed versions of this at Asian supermarkets (where you should also be able to track down the nori and shiso). And if you're anything like me, you'll soon find yourself sprinkling it onto everything: sandwiches, avocado on toast, baked fish.

TO TRANSPORT
This is a pack-and-go number: just take your boiled quail eggs in a bowl or container and your duo of dipping salts in individual jars.

Pea and mint tarts

When it comes to children's birthday parties, I am strictly a two-trick pony. My first trick is gingerbread biscuits cut out in the shape of the digit representing the child's age (see page 148). My second trick is pea tarts. I can crank them out with my eyes closed these days, and for any adult adrift in a world of fairy bread and high-pitched squealing – and, it must be admitted, sugar-loaded novelty gingerbread digits – the arrival of a grown-up savoury tartlet improves the situation no end. I use ready-made puff pastry for these, and I don't blind-bake them. Seriously, this is a fast tart. Ahem.

Makes 36

280 g (10 oz/2 cups) frozen peas, thawed
250 g (9 oz) feta, crumbled
handful of mint leaves, shredded
finely grated zest of ½ lemon
pinch of chilli flakes – optional
2 eggs
300 ml (10½ fl oz) sour cream
80 g (2¾ oz/¾ cup) finely grated parmesan
4 sheets ready-made puff pastry, thawed if frozen

Preheat the oven to 180°C (350°F) and lightly grease three shallow 12-hole mini-muffin or patty-pan tins (or make and bake these in batches if you only have one such tin).

In a bowl, mix the peas with the feta, mint and lemon zest. If you're making these for grown-ups who like things a bit hot, you could definitely add some chilli flakes at this point. In a small jug, whisk the eggs, sour cream and parmesan, then season to taste with pepper (don't worry about salt, which will be supplied in sufficient quantities by the feta and parmesan).

Now, lay out your pastry on a lightly floured surface and cut out rounds about 8 cm (3¼ in) across – you should get about 9 rounds out of each pastry sheet. You could re-roll the odds and ends but I wouldn't really recommend it, as overworked pastry gets a bit dense and shrinky. Press each round into a hole in your prepared tin, creating an instant tart case. Load each tart case with a heaping tablespoon of the pea and feta mixture, then pour in enough of the egg mixture to fill them about two-thirds full.

Slip the tarts into the oven and bake for about 15 minutes, or until puffed and golden. Check the base of the tarts to make sure that they are well browned and crisp, not pale and flabby, then cool on a wire rack.

TO TRANSPORT
Pack the cooled tarts into a basket or tin and get going.

Choosing your special delivery

New parents

The great thing about cooking for new parents is that almost anything will do. Same goes for swotting students, if you happen to have any of those to feed. A jar of walnut and red pepper dip (page 214) and a tub of winter tabbouleh (page 54) – brilliant! Bircher muesli (page 17) and a slab of chocolate beetroot cake (page 112) – just what's needed! In the early weeks, day and night blend together; any notion of what constitutes a meal and when you need to eat it, that is all lost. But appetites, especially when breastfeeding, are huge. Ask first if there are any dietary considerations (some people find that windy foods transfer through breast milk to make windy babies). Also, don't forget to look after new parents the second, third, and fourth time around because – newsflash – it doesn't get any easier. A batch of pea and mint tarts (page 218) and some spaghetti lentilaise (page 86) are a good idea for any older children in the household. Hopefully, the co-parent will be on hand for simple food collation in the first two weeks, but nevertheless, nutritious food that can be eaten with one hand (or shovelled in with a fork) is ideal: Christobel's spicy nuts (page 204), French lentil salad (page 51), or any of the papillotes (pages 82–84). Although one woman reported that a boozy trifle with a circumference as big as a bicycle wheel, dropped off soon after the birth of her third child, was the best present she'd ever received in her life. So give the sweets a spin if that's what you like cooking – macadamia, mango and lemon myrtle trifle (page 192), cherry coconut brownies (page 165), chocolate mousse (page 188), or if you really love these people, a huge tray of chocolate choux buns (page 166) for immediate consumption.

The unwell

Sometimes the best way to cook for someone who's ill is to cater for their carers and/or family. Drop off something that doesn't need much preparation, such as granola (page 16), lasagne (page 96), tomato salad spaghetti (page 95), or onion and cheddar tart (page 64).

Whether we're coping with a life-altering mental illness, or a course of chemotherapy, sometimes just knowing that the people we love are being taken care of is a huge relief. It isn't always the case that serious illness will ruin a person's appetite, but do ask what might be palatable that week. Medication, and illness, can do mighty strange things to the senses. Received wisdom suggests that, ironically, the main food to be avoided is someone's favourite dish. The association between how a once-loved meal tastes under the cloak of disrupted taste or illness might ruin the enjoyment of that dish for good. Likewise, a soup devoured one week might well taste like potage of battery acid – or nothing at all – the next. Don't be offended; do ask. And if someone is struggling to raise an appetite, go miniature: quail eggs with their dipping salts (page 216) or some goat's cheese and polenta muffins (page 213) that can be kept on standby in the freezer.

The convalescing

At no time is there a greater requirement for soup than in those few days at the end of a stinking cold or flu. Obviously, in these circumstances, you're going to be tiptoeing in and dropping something off, or discreetly preparing it for them in-between bouts of pillow-plumping. Harira (page 48), winter's consolation (page 44) and Asian pumpkin and sweet potato (page 46) are all options. Then perhaps the vegetarian 'cassoulet' (page 88) or chickpea and halloumi bake (page 90) when they are starting to get their strength back.

The bereaved

Check first that they are not wading in lamb casseroles at home. And instead think about scheduling in a food drop-off in weeks 3 or 4: the imam's moussaka (page 97) and smoked mozzarella tart (page 78) are good choices. Anecdotal evidence in these parts suggests that there is often a flurry of foodstuff in the early days, then it tails off as everyone moves on. It's like when you have a baby and you get a million things that fit a one-day-old, then by the time your kid's six months old it's living in a nappy and a slightly-too-small singlet. Grief and sorrow often outlast the fortnight.

The overwhelmed

The key thing to understand when dealing with the overwhelmed is that they can hardly even bear it when you ring up. So, for god's sake, don't go burdening them with some dish that requires them to do anything, or that cannot be frozen and will make them feel even more miserable and hopeless as they watch it slowly going off. Take something like Bircher muesli (page 17). Or spicy nuts (page 204). Or soup of any sort. Or lasagne (page 96). Or make any children in the house a batch of fairy cakes (page 114). Date and walnut bread (page 18) and apricot slice (page 118) both keep for quite a while and also freeze well.

The lucky

Okay, friends or family fresh back from their annual ski jag to Aspen might not need our sympathy, but they might well need our soup (pages 42–48) – perhaps with some bread and milk for the morning, just to get them through the jet lag and first day of post-holiday malaise. Same goes for returnees from road trips in need of something nutritious after endless Burger Rings and rivers of iced coffee: go for a 'pantry challenge' gratin (page 92), beetroot tarte tatin (page 62) or cauliflower 'rice' salad (page 102). For bridesmaids who have worked tirelessly on their sister's wedding for five straight months . . . but what is there for them the morning after? Hopefully, you – with a batch of Scandinavian cinnamon buns (page 14) and a keen appetite for tales from the reception. Or sometimes it's just nice to celebrate when you can. A new job, a new house, the long-awaited promotion, a birthday, the IVF that finally worked. Cakes are the obvious choice: try hummingbird-ish (page 110) or ginger fluff (page 138).

The unlucky

Oh no, you didn't get that job, you lost your job, your dog was hit by a car, your girlfriend bolted, your children have head lice *again*? You can't do much to fix these things, but respite can sometimes be achieved through cake (pages 106–138), cocktails (page 202) and company.

Party people

The key here is self-sufficiency. You know those parties where you slip in and everything's going full-tilt, and you can barely find a clean glass? Well, similarly, if you're taking canapés or party food – come prepared. With the Brazilian cheese puffs known as 'pao de queijo' (page 208), you take your muffin tin and your batter in a jug and do the rest on-site. Don't forget a plate for the finished product; hell, take your own oven mitts if you sense it's going to be *that* kind of a party. Clearly, the carrot and caraway cheese triangle (page 207) is very much your friend here. Cold snacks may be less fuss, but a warm pea and mint tart (page 218) will make you the most popular person in the room for at least 5 minutes. If it is a dinner or lunch party you are going to, offer to bring a course, then reach for the stars: travelling cheese soufflé (page 58), hot-smoked salmon (page 100), apple tangle cake (page 106), grape and mandarin tartlets (page 142), or itty-bitty shot glasses of lemon verbena posset (page 176).

Barbecues

Don't fall into the trap of taking a bag of sausages. Take something no-one else will – like a Thai green curry (page 98)! Or some barbecued eggplant smash to have with pitta crisps (page 56) and fattoush (page 52). For dessert time, fruit datschi (page 134) caters for many, and is dead easy to transport. A vacherin (page 158), chocolate pomegranate cloud cake (page 120), or the hummingbird-ish cake (page 110) are also likely to be crowd-pleasers.

Acknowledgements

Annabel

My first thanks are to Wendy Sharpe, my talented co-author, without whose imagination – not to mention frenzied testing, tasting and twiddling – this book could never have taken shape the way it did, in what seemed like a consternatingly brief timeframe. Thank you for all that work, and for the mango in Year Three, and for everything in between. The thing I love most about you is that you are still reduced to tears by the sight of a left-behind packed lunch.

My mum, Christobel, taught me how to cook. But the best thing I inherited from her, I reckon, was her love of cooking for others, and the enthusiasm with which she squirrels away recipes and ideas for experimentation when the moment arises. My granny, Sheila Riggs, has the same trait, as do my aunties Liz Coles and Jenny Bradley, at whose homes I have eaten many delicious things. My brothers James and Tom love a bit of kitchen invention too – so thanks, Mum. And Dad, who taught us the finer points of crabbing (and yes, we do realise how hilarious that is, very good). South Australian blue swimmer crabs, cooked and rolled up in newspaper, with a bottle of vinegar on the side, are the ultimate moveable feast. Thank you to the Two Wells community, too, which gave Wendy and me a great place to grow up.

There are so many people whose food – transportable and otherwise – has influenced the way I cook. I would love to thank you all, but it would take too long; I might just pop round with some biscuits.

Thank you to my employer, the ABC, for giving me an opportunity to incorporate my love of cooking into my actual job. Thank you to the *Kitchen Cabinet* team, who make it so much fun, and to the politicians who keep letting us in.

And to my beloved little family – Jeremy, Audrey, Elliott and Kate: nothing makes me happier than to cook for you. Or with you. My mum once told me that the sound of little chairs being dragged up to help at the kitchen bench was the loveliest sound there is, and now I know exactly what she meant.

Wendy

I came to love cooking through my love of eating. And the best food was from the kitchen of my grandmother, Gwen Bennett, a skilled and generous cook whose meals were enjoyed by so many. Much of the how and why I cook is because of her. I would also like to thank the people who, in big and small ways, helped me reach the finish line on this project: my parents, Patricia and John Sharpe; the family and friends who had me to stay, drove me about and cooked nice meals while I was in Sydney; Annie and Matt Braithwaite-Young; my lovely friends in London W3, always ready to cheerlead, taste-test and lend practical and moral support, especially Rachel and Jon Westall, Sarah Collinson, Belinda Fowler and Phoebe Barran. And, in France, Agnes Borderie and her family.

A big shout-out to all the people who like to talk about food and who exchange recipes with me, but in particular those who generously shared dishes with Annabel and me for this book: Christobel Crabb, Michael Jenkins, my clever cooking aunts Bronwyn Sharpe and Jeanette Sharpe, cousin Miranda Bennett, Elmar and Daniella Lohler, and Vanessa Galbraith. I would also like to shine a light on the extended Delaunay family and Beatrice Chevrin, who showed me so much about how to cook, and, with Remy, taught me through exquisite demonstration about *l'art de recevoir. Merci.*

Thank you also to Zoë Mullan, for her continued support in my day job.

To my co-author, AC, thank you for having faith in me and sticking by me, and for about 35 years of food exchange.

A huge thank you to Alice, Louis and Felix Jenkins, who were so enthusiastic about this project from the beginning to the slightly messy end, and who put up with a lot of distracted parenting while I was getting it done. Thank you for not being fussy eaters; you three brighten every day, and I love cooking for you. And, of course, thank you to and for my husband, Michael Jenkins, who never runs out of love, sense, encouragement, patience or appetite. No-one was more committed to taste-testing than he! Thank you, thank you.

The authors would like to thank Murdoch Books, and publisher Jane Morrow – both for her instant enthusiasm for the idea of travelling food, and for honouring the book's spirit of friendship. Alison Cowan did a fine job of corralling and keeping track of copy, and making sensible suggestions: thank you. Photographing this book was enormously good fun, thanks to the talents and fine company of Rob Palmer and Michelle 'Let's just finish this off with some crumbs' Noerianto. Absolutely indispensable on the photo shoot was the fabulous and knowledgeable Tracey Meharg, who was focussed, organised and cheerful for two straight weeks. She sourced all the ingredients for, and with, the two of us – and cooked many of the dishes you see photographed here. Thank you to the designers who made this book beautiful, under the supervision of Megan Pigott. And to Virginia Birch, Christine Farmer and Matt Hoy. And to Fiona Inglis, of Curtis Brown, whose counsel has been invaluable throughout.

Index

Page numbers in italics refer to photographs

227

Published in 2015 by Murdoch Books, an imprint of Allen & Unwin

Murdoch Books Australia
83 Alexander Street
Crows Nest NSW 2065
Phone: +61 (0) 2 8425 0100
Fax: +61 (0) 2 9906 2218
murdochbooks.com.au
info@murdochbooks.com.au

Murdoch Books UK
Erico House, 6th Floor
93–99 Upper Richmond Road
Putney, London SW15 2TG
Phone: +44 (0) 20 8785 5995
murdochbooks.co.uk
info@murdochbooks.co.uk

For Corporate Orders & Custom Publishing contact
Noel Hammond, National Business Development Manager, Murdoch Books Australia

Publisher: Jane Morrow
Editorial Manager: Virginia Birch
Design Manager and Cover Designer: Megan Pigott
Editor: Alison Cowan
Designer: Arielle Gamble
Photographer: Rob Palmer
Stylist: Michelle Noerianto
Home Economist: Tracey Meharg
Production Manager: Mary Bjelobrk

A cataloguing-in-publication entry is available from the catalogue of the National Library of Australia at nla.gov.au.

ISBN 978 1 74336 619 6 Australia
ISBN 978 1 74336 620 2 UK

A catalogue record for this book is available from the British Library.

Colour reproduction by Splitting Image Colour Studio Pty Ltd, Clayton, Victoria
Printed by 1010 Printing International Limited, China

IMPORTANT: Those who might be at risk from the effects of salmonella poisoning (the elderly, pregnant women, young children and those suffering from immune deficiency diseases) should consult their doctor with any concerns about eating raw eggs.

OVEN GUIDE: You may find cooking times vary depending on the oven you are using. For fan-forced ovens, as a general rule, set the oven temperature to 20°C (35°F) lower than indicated in the recipe.

MEASURES GUIDE: We have used 20 ml (4 teaspoon) tablespoon measures. If you are using a 15 ml (3 teaspoon) tablespoon add an extra teaspoon of the ingredient for each tablespoon specified.